춘향전

The Story of Chunhyang

머리말

　"다락원 한국어 학습문고" 시리즈는 대표적인 한국 문학 작품을 한국어 학습자들의 읽기 수준에 맞도록 재구성하여 쉽고 재미있게 독해력을 증진할 수 있도록 하였습니다. '국제 통용 한국어 표준 교육 과정'과 '한국어 교육 어휘 내용 개발'을 기준으로 초급부터 고급(A1~C2)으로 구분하여 지문을 읽으면서 각자의 수준에 맞는 필수 어휘와 표현을 자연스럽게 익힐 수 있습니다.

　시대적 배경과 관련된 어휘에는 별도의 설명을 추가하여 그 당시 문화에 대해 이해하면서 본문을 읽을 수 있도록 하였습니다. 더불어 의미 전달에 충실한 번역문과 내용 이해 문제를 수록하여 자신의 이해 정도를 점검하고 확인할 수 있도록 하였고, 전문 성우가 직접 낭독한 음원을 통해 눈과 귀를 동시에 활용한 독해 연습이 가능하도록 하였습니다.

　"다락원 한국어 학습문고" 시리즈를 통해 보다 유익하고 재미있는 한국어 학습이 되시길 바랍니다.

다락원 한국어 학습문고
저자 대표 **김유미**

Preface

The Darakwon Korean Readers series adapts the most well-known Korean literary works to the reading levels of Korean language learners, restructuring them into simple and fun stories that encourage the improvement of reading comprehension skills. Based on the "International Standard Curriculum for the Korean Language" and "Research on Korean Language Education Vocabulary Content Development", the texts have been graded from beginner to advanced levels (A1–C2) so that readers can naturally learn the necessary vocabulary and expressions that match their level.

With supplementary explanations concerning historical background, learners can understand the culture of the era as they read. In addition, students can assess and confirm their understanding with the included reading comprehension questions and translations faithful to the meaning of the original text. Recordings of the stories by professional voice actors also allow reading practice through the simultaneous use of learners' eyes and ears.

We hope that the Darakwon Korean Readers series will provide learners with a more fruitful and interesting Korean language learning experience.

Darakwon Korean Readers
Kim Yu Mi, Lead Author

일러두기

How to Use This Book

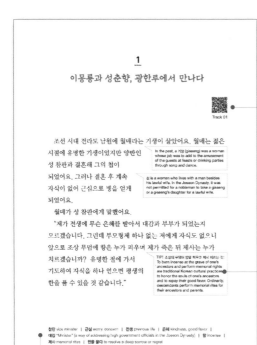

듣기 Listening

QR 코드를 통해 전문 성우가 녹음한 정확하고 생생한 작품 낭독을 들을 수 있습니다.

Using the corresponding QR codes, learners can access professional recordings of the story.

해설 Notes

학습자들이 내용을 이해하는 데 필요한 한국어 문법, 표현, 어휘, 속담, 문화적 배경 등을 알기 쉽게 설명해 주어 별도로 사전을 찾을 필요가 없도록 하였습니다.

Explanations of essential Korean grammar, expressions, vocabulary, proverbs, cultural background, etc. are provided to learners to aid understanding without the need to consult a separate dictionary.

어휘 설명 Vocabulary Explanation

각 권의 수준에 맞춰 본문에서 꼭 알아야 하는 필수 어휘를 영어 번역과 함께 제시하였습니다.

English translations are provided for the essential vocabulary matched to the level of each title.

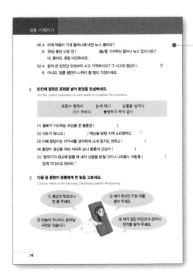

내용 이해하기 Reading Comprehension

다양한 문제를 통해 본문 내용 이해와 함께 해당 레벨에서 알아야 할 문형과 어휘를 다시 한번 확인할 수 있습니다.

Learners can check their understanding of the main text while also reviewing the essential sentence patterns and vocabulary for their level through various comprehension questions.

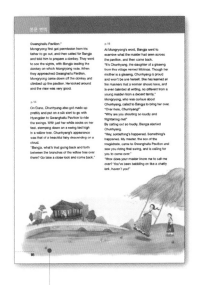

본문 번역 Text Translations

한국어 본문 내용을 정확히 이해할 수 있도록 의미 전달에 충실한 영어 번역을 수록하였습니다.

An English translation faithful to the original text is included to ensure an exact understanding of the original Korean story.

모범 답안 Answers

모범 답안과 비교하며 자신의 이해 정도를 스스로 평가하고 진단할 수 있습니다.

Learners can self-evaluate and assess their level of understanding by comparing their answers to the answer key.

작품 소개

춘향전

"춘향전"은 열여섯 살 청춘인 춘향과 몽룡의 신분을 뛰어넘은 사랑 이야기로, 동화, 드라마, 영화 등으로 다양하게 접할 수 있기 때문에 한국에서 이들의 이야기를 모르는 사람은 거의 없을 것입니다.

소설 "춘향전"은 판소리에서 발전하여 글로 옮기는 과정에서 특정한 작가 없이 옮기는 사람의 의도나 지역에 따라 조금씩 내용이 달라졌습니다. 이 때문에 다양한 춘향의 모습이 전해지고 있는데 그중에서도 전라도 지방의 〈열녀춘향수절가〉가 가장 대중적으로 알려져 있습니다.

"춘향전"을 흔히 한국의 '로미오와 줄리엣'이라고 부르는 것은 이루어질 수 없는 사이에 있는 남녀의 사랑 이야기이기 때문입니다. "춘향전"에는 청춘 남녀의 만남과 사랑, 신분 차이로 인한 이별, 극적인 만남이 생생하게 담겨 있습니다. 춘향이 몽룡을 얼마나 믿고 기다렸는지, 몽룡은 춘향과의 약속을 지키기 위해 어떤 노력을 했는지를 통해 깊은 감동을 느낄 수 있습니다.

이 소설의 마지막에 춘향은 몽룡의 정실부인이 되고 왕이 인정한 정렬부인이 됩니다. 정렬부인은 행실이 바르고 절개가 굳은 부인에게 왕이 내리는 이름인데 당시 기생의 딸은 결코 받을 수 없었습니다. 그러나 소설에서는 춘향의 사랑이 승리하는 결말을 그려서 많은 사람들의 공감을 받았습니다. "춘향전"을 통해 신분을 초월한 남녀의 사랑과 지배층의 폭력에 굴하지 않는 서민들의 용기를 읽을 수 있습니다.

Introduction to the Story

The Story of Chunhyang

"The Story of Chunhyang" is a story about the love of 16-year-old youth Chunhyang and Mongryong that overcomes their differences in social standing, and because their story can be found in various formats, including fairy tales, TV dramas, movies, and more, there are few in Korea who aren't familiar with it.

The novel "The Story of Chunhyang" evolved from pansori into writing, and along the way, as it had no specific author, the content of the story changed bit by bit depending on who told it and where it was being told. Because of this, Chunhyang is described in various ways. Among the many versions, Jeolla-do Province's "Yeollyeo Chunhyang Sujeol Ga (The Faithful Story of Virtuous Chunhyang)" is the most popularly known.

"The Story of Chunhyang" is often called "Korea's Romeo and Juliet" because it's a story of the love of a man and woman that can never be realized. Contained in vivid detail within "The Story of Chunhyang" are the meeting and love story of a young man and woman, their farewell due to differences in social standing, and their dramatic reunion. It's deeply touching as it conveys how much Chunhyang trusted and waited for Mongryong, and how hard Mongryong worked to keep his promise to Chunhyang.

At the end of this story, Chunhyang becomes Mongryong's lawful wife and is recognized by the king as a "Lady of Virtue." This title was bestowed by the king upon proper and chaste women, but in those days, could never be received by the daughter of a gisaeng. But as the novel depicts an ending in which Chunhyang's love conquers all, many people identified with it. Through "The Story of Chunhyang," you'll be able to read a story in which the love of a man and a woman transcends their social status, and the courage of the peasants rises above violence by the ruling class.

목차
Table of Contents

춘향전

The Story of Chunhyang

등장인물
Characters

성춘향
Seong Chunhyang

기생 월매의 딸로 예쁘고
글재주가 좋다. 결혼을 약속한
이몽룡만을 사랑한다.

The daughter of the
gisaeng Wolmae. She is
beautiful and has a talent
for writing. She loves only
Lee Mongryong, who has
promised to marry her.

이몽룡
Lee Mongryong

남원 사또의 아들로 춘향을
만나 첫눈에 반한다. 춘향과
헤어져 한양으로 가지만 춘향
을 다시 만난다.

The son of the magistrate
of Namwon. He falls in love
with Chunhyang at first sight.
He parts with Chunhyang
to go to Hanyang(the
old name for Seoul) but
reunites with her.

향단
Hyangdan

춘향의 몸종으로 착하다.
변 사또에게 괴롭힘을 당하는
춘향이를 잘 보살펴 준다.

Chunhyang's kind
handmaiden. She watches
out for Chunhyang, who is
tormented by Magistrate
Byeon.

방자
Bangja

이몽룡의 몸종으로 눈치가
빠르다. 몽룡이 춘향을 몰래
만나러 다니도록 도와준다.

Lee Mongryong's quick-
witted servant. He helps
Mongryong to meet
Chunhyang in secret.

월매
Wolmae

춘향의 엄마이다. 기생이었지
만 성 참판과 살며 춘향을
낳는다. 춘향을 소중하게
생각하며 곱게 키운다.

Chunhyang's mother.
She was a gisaeng, but
while living with Vice
Minister Seong, gives
birth to Chunhyang. She
considers Chunhyang as
very precious and raises
her well.

변학도
Byeon Hakdo

남원에 새로 온 사또로 백성들
을 돌보지 않는다. 춘향의 아름
다움에 빠져 춘향을 괴롭힌다.

The newly arrived
magistrate of Namwon
who doesn't look after
his subjects. He falls for
Chunhyang's beauty and
torments her.

1

이몽룡과 성춘향, 광한루에서 만나다

Track 01

조선 시대 전라도 남원에 월매라는 기생이 살았어요. 월매는 젊은 시절에 유명한 기생이었지만 양반인 성 참판과 결혼해 그의 첩이 되었어요. 그러나 결혼 후 계속 자식이 없어 근심으로 병을 얻게 되었어요.

> In the past, a 기생 (gisaeng) was a woman whose job was to add to the amusement of the guests at feasts or drinking parties through song and dance.

> 첩 is a woman who lives with a man besides his lawful wife. In the Joseon Dynasty, it was not permitted for a nobleman to take a gisaeng or a gisaeng's daughter for a lawful wife.

월매가 성 참판에게 말했어요.

"제가 전생에 무슨 은혜를 받아서 대감과 부부가 되었는지 모르겠습니다. 그런데 부모형제 하나 없는 저에게 자식도 없으니 앞으로 조상 무덤에 향은 누가 피우며 제가 죽은 뒤 제사는 누가 치르겠습니까? 유명한 절에 가서 기도하여 자식을 하나 얻으면 평생의 한을 풀 수 있을 것 같습니다."

> TIP! 조상의 무덤에 향을 피우고 제사 치르는 것: To burn incense at the grave of one's ancestors and perform memorial rights are traditional Korean cultural practices to honor the souls of one's ancestors and to repay their good favor. Ordinarily, descendants perform memorial rites for their ancestors and parents.

참판 vice minister | 근심 worry, concern | 전생 previous life | 은혜 kindness, good favor | 대감 "Minister" (a way of addressing high government officials in the Joseon Dynasty) | 향 incense | 제사 memorial rites | 한을 풀다 to resolve a deep sorrow or regret

이날부터 성 참판 부부는 전국의 유명한 산을 돌며 백일 동안 신령님에게 빌고 또 빌었어요.

"신령님, 부디 아이 하나만 낳게 해 주세요."

그들의 정성이 하늘에 닿았는지 열 달 후, 월매는 예쁜 딸을 낳았어요. 월매는 딸을 '봄 향기'라는 의미의 춘향이라고 부르며 보석처럼 귀하게 키웠어요. 춘향은 어릴 때부터 책을 좋아해서 글재주가 뛰어났고 점점 더 예의 바르고 예쁘게 자랐어요. 그래서 남원에서 춘향을 모르는 사람은 아무도 없었어요.

> 보석처럼: 보석 is a precious and expensive stone, so this means that Chunhyang was treasured and looked after with care, like one might care for a jewel. "N+처럼" is used when making a comparison.

한편 한양에는 이한림이라는 양반이 살았어요. 그는 조상 때부터 벼슬을 한 유명한 집안의 사람이었고 아들이 하나 있었어요. 아들의 이름을 꿈을 의미하는 '몽'과 용을 의미하는 '룡'이라는 이몽룡이라고 지었는데, 이한림의 아내가 몽룡을 낳기 전에 용꿈을 꾸었기 때문이었어요. 몽룡의 나이는 열여섯 살이고 부모 말씀을 잘 듣고 글재주도 좋았어요.

> A dream that occurs when a child is conceived is called 태몽 (taemong, a conception dream), and the sex and future prospects of the child are interpreted from the dream. A conception dream in which a dragon appears is analyzed as meaning the child will be well-learned or become a scholar in a high government position.

신령님 spirits, gods | 정성 sincerity, devotion | 귀하다 to be precious, to be valuable | 글재주 talent for writing | 예의 바르다 to be polite, to be well-mannered | 양반 nobleman | 조상 ancestor | 벼슬 government position | 용 dragon

어느 날 몽룡이 하인인 방자를 불렀어요.

"방자야, 남원에서 경치가 좋은 곳이 어디냐?"

"공부하시는 도련님이 경치 좋은 곳을 찾아 뭐 하시게요?"

> An ending suffix that speaks down to another party, used when expressing a question (-느냐, -냐, -니, -지). In the past, it was mainly used by noblemen when they spoke to those beneath them.

"그건 네가 몰라서 하는 말이다. 옛날부터 최고의 학자들이 경치 좋은 곳에 가서 구경하며 공부하지 않았더냐? 게다가 오늘은 단오가 아니냐? 잔소리 말고 어서 추천해 보아라."

> V/A + -더-: Indicates that one is recalling, from the present, a fact from the past that was learned through personal experience.
>
> TIP! 단오(Dano), which falls on the 5th day of the 5th month of the lunar calendar, is a holiday during which people make and eat Dano rice cakes, women wash their hair in water infused with irises and play on swings, and men wrestle.

방자는 몽룡에게 남원의 경치 좋은 곳을 소개했어요.

"남원의 경치는 동쪽으로 가시면 선원사가 좋고, 서쪽으로는 관왕묘가, 남쪽에는 광한루 오작교, 영주각이 좋고, 북쪽에는 교룡산성이 좋으니 도련님이 가시고 싶은 곳을 정하십시오."

"음, 광한루 오작교로 가자."

몽룡은 먼저 아버지께 외출 허락을 받고 방자를 불러 당나귀를 준비시켰어요. 몽룡이 탄 당나귀를 방자가 끌고 구경 나갔어요. 광한루 근처에 도착했을 때 몽룡은 당나귀에서 내려 광한루에 올라갔어요. 주위를 살펴보니 경치가 아주 좋았어요.

도련님 young master, gentleman, lord (a title given in the past to young men of high status) |
학자 scholar | 잔소리 nagging, scolding | 추천하다 to recommend | 당나귀 donkey

춘향도 단오에 그네를 타려고 예쁘게 화장하고 비단 치마를
입고 향단이와 같이 광한루에 갔어요. 하얀 버선만 신고 버드나무
높은 곳에 매여 있는 그네 위에서 발을 구르는 춘향의 모습이 마치
선녀가 구름을 타고 내려오는 듯

발을 구르다: Here, 구르다 means to step firmly and push down with one's foot on the board of the swing.

아름다웠어요.

　"방자야, 저 건너 버드나무 가지 사이로 오락가락하는 하는 것이
무엇이냐? 자세히 보고 오너라."

화장하다 to put on make-up, to get made up | 비단 silk | 버선 Korean-style socks |
버드나무 willow tree | 오락가락하다 to go back and forth

광한루에서 건너편을 바라보던 몽룡의 말에 방자가 살펴보고
돌아왔어요.

"이 마을 기생 월매의 딸 춘향입니다. 비록 어미가 기생이지만
춘향이는 콧대가 높아 기생을 하지 않고 여자가 갖춰야 할 예절을 다
배우고 글재주까지 뛰어나 여염집
규수와 다름없습니다."

> 콧대(가) 높다: (literally, to have a high nose)
> Used to describe someone who puts on
> airs or considers themself important.

> 여염집 규수: A polite term used to
> address an unmarried woman from
> an ordinary commoner's home.

춘향이 궁금한 몽룡은 방자를 불러
춘향을 여기로 데리고 오라고 했어요.

"여봐라, 춘향아!"

"왜 그렇게 크게 소리쳐서 사람을 놀라게 해!"

방자가 크게 부르는 바람에 춘향은 깜짝 놀랐어요.

"얘, 일 났다. 일 났어.
사또의 아들인 우리

> V + -는 바람에: Indicates that the action or state in the
> preceding clause describes the cause or reason for the
> following clause.

도련님이 광한루에 오셨다가 너 그네 타는 것을 보고 불러오란다."

"도련님이 나를 어떻게 알고 부른단 말이냐? 네가 종달새처럼
수다스럽게 종알거렸구나!"

"아니다, 아니야. 이건 네 탓이야. 계집아이가 그네를 타려면
조용히 집 안에서 탈 것이지,

> 계집아이: An informal term for a
> young woman.

사람들 다 모이는 광한루에서 탈 건 뭐란
말이냐. 그 모습을 보고 도련님이 첫눈에 반했으니 어서 건너가자."

비록 even if, although | 어미 mother | 다름없다 to be similar to, to be no different from | 소리치다
to shout | 종달새 lark | 수다스럽다 to be talkative, to be chatty | 종알거리다 to chatter, to babble |
첫눈에 반하다 to fall in love at first sight

"오늘은 단오가 아니냐? 다른 집 처녀들도 그네를 타고 있고.
또 내가 기생 딸이긴 하지만, 여염집 여자인데 함부로 오라고
부르다니……. 난 갈 수 없다."

방자가 몽룡에게 이 말을 그대로 전하자 몽룡의 마음은 더욱
춘향에게 끌렸어요.

"도련님이 말씀하시기를, '내가 춘향을 기생으로 여기는 것이
아니라 글을 잘한다기에 부르는 것이다. 여염집 여자를 부르는 것이
이상하기는 하나

> V/A + -기에: Indicates a cause or basis for the following clause.

잘못이라 생각지 말고 잠시 다녀가면 어떤가?' 하신다."

그 말을 듣고 춘향이 못 이기는 체하며 방자를 따라 몽룡이 있는
광한루로 갔어요.

> V/A + -는 체하다: Indicates that an action or state is disguised with a lie that is different from the actual truth.

춘향은 누각에 사뿐사뿐 걸어
올라가 몽룡에게 인사했어요. 몽룡은 고운 태도로 단정히 앉는
춘향의 모습을 보고 이렇게 생각했어요.

'마치 하늘나라의 선녀가 남원 땅에 내려온 것 같구나! 춘향의
얼굴과 태도가 이 세상 사람이 아니구나!'

춘향 또한 몽룡을 살펴보니 외모가 남달랐어요. 두 눈썹 사이가
높으니 이름을 널리 알릴 것이요, 이마, 코, 턱, 광대뼈가 잘 어울려
모였으니 크게 될 사람 같았어요.
춘향은 몽룡을 보고 첫눈에 반해
부끄러워 고개를 숙였어요.

> • 관상 (physiognomy): The practice of judging someone's destiny, personality, life expectancy, etc. by examining their face. This passage is talking about the physiognomy of Mongryong.
> • 크게 되다: Means to succeed in the future; that one's name will become well-known.

함부로 recklessly, thoughtlessly | 끌리다 to be drawn toward | 여기다 to regard, to consider |
누각 pavilion, building with many stories | 곱다 to be beautiful, to be lovely | 외모가 남다르다 to have
extraordinary looks | 이마 forehead | 턱 chin | 광대뼈 cheek bones | 숙이다 to bow, to bend

"네 성은 무엇이고 나이는 몇 살이냐?"

"성은 성가이고 나이는 열여섯입니다."

"허허, 네 나이 나와 동갑이구나! 성은 나와 다르니 하늘이 인연을 맺어 준 것이 분명하다. 부모님은 다 살아 계시냐?"

> In traditional society, if two people had the same family name, they couldn't marry as they were family. This is expressing that Chunhyang and Mongryong, who are of similar age and have different family names, were a match made in heaven.

"어머니만 계시고, 어머니에게 자식은 저 하나뿐입니다."

"외동딸이로구나. 춘향아, 우리가 하늘이 정해 준 인연으로 만났으니 평생 같이 살아 보자꾸나."

"오늘 처음 만났는데 어찌하여 우리가 인연이란 말씀입니까?

> V + −자꾸나: An ending suffix that is used to suggest performing an action together. Provides a bit more intimacy than −자.

도련님은 양반 댁 자식이고, 저는 천한 첩의 자식인데, 제가 마음을 준 후 도련님께서 저를 버리시면 저는 어떻게 살아갈 수 있겠습니까? 그런 말씀 하지 마세요."

"그런 말 하지 말거라. 나는 너와 결혼하여 부부가 될 것이다. 오늘 밤 내가 너의 집에 갈 것이니 반갑게 맞이해 주면 좋겠구나."

동갑 the same age | 인연을 맺다 to bond, to tie together | 외동딸 only daughter | 어찌하다 how, "what to do" | 천하다 to be low, to be humble | 맞이하다 to receive, to welcome

<u>2</u>
몽룡과 춘향, 결혼을 약속하다

Track 02

춘향과 헤어져 집에 돌아온 몽룡은 책을 폈지만, 책 내용은
머릿속에 들어오지 않고 춘향 생각만 났어요. 몽룡은 해가 지기를
목이 빠지게 기다렸어요. 날이 어두워지자 몽룡이 벌떡 일어났어요.

"방자야! 어서 춘향이네 집으로
안내하거라."

> • 목이 빠지게 기다리다: Means to wait very impatiently.
> • V + –자: A connector that indicates that events or actions occur one after another.

몽룡이 방자를 따라 춘향의 집에
도착했어요. 방자는 춘향의 방에 있는 창문 밑으로 가서 춘향을
불렀어요. 춘향은 깜짝 놀라 건넌방에 있는 어머니를 깨웠어요.

"어머니, 방자가 도련님을 모시고 왔습니다."

월매는 그 말을 듣고 향단이를 불렀어요.

"향단아! 방을 정리하고 불을 켜라."

급히 방에서 나오는 월매는 나이 오십이 넘었지만, 외모가
단정하고 여전히 아름다웠어요. 춘향이 아름다운 건 어머니를
닮았기 때문이었어요.

벌떡 suddenly | **건넌방** room opposite another, (in a traditional Korean house) room across the main hall from the main room of the house | **여전히** still, as ever

월매는 두 손을 모으고 몽룡을 공손히 맞이했어요.

"도련님, 안녕하십니까?"

"자네가 춘향이 어미인가? 자네도 잘 지냈는가?"

"네, 귀하신 도련님이 저희 집에 와 주시니 어떻게 대접해야 할지 모르겠습니다."

> 자네: A term used to elevate a friend or someone of a lower social standing. Mongryong, the son of a nobleman, is younger than Wolmae, but his status is higher, so he is using a polite word to elevate her subordinate to him.

월매는 몽룡을 방으로 모셔 차와 담배를 권한 후 춘향을 불렀어요. 춘향은 조용히 들어와 부끄러워하며 서 있었어요.

"낮에 우연히 광한루에서 춘향을 보고 첫눈에 반해 나비가 꽃을 찾듯이 이렇게 왔네. 춘향과 결혼을 하고 싶은데 자네 생각은 어떠한가?"

"도련님, 소인이 젊었을 때 성 참판 영감이 한양에서 잠시 남원에 내려왔지요. 그때 수청을 들라는 명령을 어기지 못해 그분을 모셨지요.

> 소인: A lowered way for a person of low standing to refer to themselves when speaking to a person of higher standing.

그러나 석 달 만에 한양으로 떠나시고 그 후 저는 딸 춘향을 얻었습니다. 하지만 참판 영감이

> 수청을 들다: Means to follow a superior administrator's orders; for a gisaeng, to offer her body to a local government officer. Here, it means to offer up one's body.

춘향의 얼굴도 보지 못하고 세상을 떠나 소인이 혼자 지금까지 춘향을 키우고 있습니다.

공손히 politely | 대접하다 to receive, to welcome someone | 권하다 to offer | 명령 order, command

그래도 뼈대 있는 집안의 아이인데 제가 부족하여 열여섯 살이 될
때까지 시집을 못 보냈지요.

> 뼈대(가) 있다: High social status or position going back generations within a family.

도련님, 순간의 감정으로
결혼한다고 하시는데, 그런 말씀 마시고 그냥 차 한잔하시고
가십시오.”

　월매는 사실 몽룡의 진심을 알기 위해 속마음과 다른 말을 했어요.

　“월매, 부모님 모셔 놓고 결혼식은 못 올리지만, 양반의 자식이
한 입으로 두말하겠는가? 내 춘향을 첫 아내같이 여길 테니
걱정하지 말고 허락해 주게.”

> • 한 입으로 두말하다: (proverb) (literally, to say two things with one mouth) To say two different things about the same subject.
> • 첫 아내같이 여기다: Means that though Chunhyang cannot become Mongryong's lawful wife, he will treat her preciously as if she were indeed his lawful wife.

　월매는 잠시 생각하더니 기분 좋게
승낙했어요.

　“이제 우리 춘향이는 도련님의
짝이 되었습니다. 저도 도련님을 내 사위로 알겠습니다.
향단아, 어서 술상 준비하거라.”

　춘향이 몽룡에게 술을 가득 부어 올리자 몽룡이 잔을 앞에 두고
말했어요.

　“내가 예를 갖춰 결혼식을 치르지 못해 미안하구나. 춘향아,
이 술을 결혼의 약속으로 알고 마시자.”

> In a traditional Korean wedding ceremony, the bride and groom share a drink from the same cup of alcohol.

순간 instant, moment ｜ 진심 genuine, sincerity ｜ 속마음 inner thoughts, true feelings ｜ 승낙하다
to approve, to consent ｜ 짝 match, pair ｜ 사위 son-in-law ｜ 붓다 to pour ｜ 치르다 to hold, to have,
to carry out

부부의 인연을 맺은 후 몽룡은 춘향의 집을 자기 집처럼 자주 드나들었어요. 처음에는 부끄러워 얼굴만 붉히던 춘향도 웃음을 보였어요. 몽룡은 넘치는 사랑을 참지 못해 노래를 불렀어요.

이리 오너라 업고 놀자, 사랑 사랑 내 사랑이야.
사랑이로구나, 내 사랑이야.

"얘, 춘향아. 우리 업기 놀이나 하자. 이리 와 업히어라."
춘향은 부끄러워 가만히 있다가 못 이기는 척 업혔어요.

> 업히다 (to be carried): The passive verb form of 업다 (to carry). Verbs become passive verbs by affixing −이−, −히−, −리−, or −기−.

"아구, 아주 무겁구나! 내 등에 업히니 기분이 어떠하냐?"
"너무너무 좋아요."

두 사람이 노래하고 업고 업히고 노는 사이에 시간은 빠르게 지났어요. 열여섯 살 두 사람이 만나 세월 가는 줄 몰랐던 것이지요.

드나들다 to frequent, to come and go | 붉히다 to blush | 넘치다 to overflow | 등 back | 세월 time

3
춘향, 몽룡과 이별하다

Track 03

1년의 시간이 지났어요. 그날도 춘향과 몽룡은 서로에게 푹 빠져 놀고 있었는데 방자가 급히 왔어요.

"도련님! 도련님! 사또께서 부르십니다."

몽룡이 서둘러 집에 가 보니 한양에서 사또 앞으로 명령이 내려왔어요.

"몽룡아, 임금께서 한양으로 올라와 더 높은 벼슬을 받고 일하라고 하시는구나. 나는 남은 일을 처리하고 갈 테니, 너는 어머니를 모시고 내일 한양으로 떠나거라."

몽룡은 아버지의 승진 소식이 기뻤지만 춘향과 헤어질 생각을 하면 팔다리에 힘이 풀리고 속이 타서 눈물이 흘렀어요.

"아니, 왜 우느냐? 평생 남원에서 살 줄 알았느냐? 좋은 일로 한양 가는 것이니 섭섭하게 생각하지 말고 떠날 준비를 하여라."

> • 힘이 풀리다: Means for energy or tension to be released.
> • 속이 타다: Means to be nervous to the point that one has butterflies in one's stomach.

빠지다 to be preoccupied with something and unable to pull oneself away | **처리하다** to handle, to take care of | **승진** promotion | **평생** lifetime, one's whole life

아버지의 얘기를 들은 후 몽룡은 방으로 들어가 어머니께
춘향과의 사이를 고백했어요. 하지만 어머니께 꾸중만 실컷 듣고
말았어요.

몽룡은 춘향에게 이 사실을 알리려고 춘향의 집으로 가는 동안
눈물이 흐르는 것을 애써 참았어요. 그러다 춘향을 보자 그만 울음이
터져 버렸어요. 춘향은 깜짝 놀라 물었어요.

"서방님, 무슨 일입니까? 울지 마시고 이유를 말씀해 보세요."

"아버님께서 승진하셔서 한양으로 가신단다."

> 서방님: A polite term for a wife to call her husband.

"정말요? 그럼 좋은 일인데 왜 우십니까?"

"우리가 헤어져야 해서……. 아버님께는 차마 말하지 못하고
어머니께 여쭈었더니 불같이 화를 내시더구나. 양반의 자식이
아버지 따라 지방에 왔다가 부인도 맞이하기 전에 첩을 얻으면 누가
좋게 보겠느냐고 하셨다. 앞길이 막히고 벼슬도 못 할 수 있으니
지금은 이렇게 이별할 수밖에
없겠구나."

> 앞길이 막히다: 앞길 is the path one's life will take in the future. If that path is blocked, it means you will be unable to do what you plan to in the future.

춘향은 몽룡에게 사정을 듣자마자 화가 났어요. 그리고는 자기
신세를 억울해하며 울었어요.

"모두 소용없구나. 이렇게 쉽게 헤어질 수도 있다는 것을 모르고
내 마음을 다 주었구나. 아이고 내 신세야."

월매가 춘향의 울음소리를 듣고 사랑싸움을 하는가 싶어서
문밖에서 한참 들어 보았는데 사랑싸움이 아니라 이별 이야기라서
깜짝 놀랐어요.

꾸중 scolding | 실컷 at length, to one's limit, to one's heart's content | 애쓰다 to work, to try hard |
그러다 and then | 차마 cannot bear (to do something) | 사정 situation, circumstances | 신세 one's
life / circumstances | 억울하다 to be unfair | 소용없다 to be of no use, to be futile | 울음소리 crying
sound | 한참 for some time

그리고 바로 문을 열고 방 안으로 달려 들어갔어요.

"아이고, 동네 사람들! 오늘 우리 집에서 사람 둘이 죽습니다."

월매가 소리치며 춘향을 붙잡았어요.

"춘향아, 우리 같이 죽자. 우리 죽은 몸이라도 도련님이 들고 가게 어서 죽자."

> N + (이)라도: Indicates that something isn't the best option out of several, but is good enough.

월매가 가슴을 치며 몽룡에게 달려들었어요.

"내 딸 춘향이를 버리고 간다니 춘향이가 무슨 죄가 있다고……. 춘향이가 무엇이 부족하오? 춘향이가 도련님을 그리워하다가 죽기라도 하면, 이 몸은 누구를 믿고 살아야 하오. 애고, 서러워라, 애고, 무서워라!"

> 애고: A shortened form of the exclamation 아이고, a sound usually made when hurt or in a difficult and confounding situation.

"장모, 너무 서러워하지 마오. 나중에 춘향이를 데려가면 그만 아니오."

곁에서 몽룡을 바라보던 춘향이 월매를 달랬어요.

"어머니, 서방님을 너무 조르지 마세요. 아마도 이번엔 헤어질 수밖에 없을 것 같네요. 한양 가서 자리 잡으면 나중에 저를 꼭 데리고 가라고 부탁이나 해 주세요."

> 자리를 잡다: Means to find a new place to live, or to establish oneself to a certain status.

춘향의 말을 듣고 월매는 몽룡에게 춘향을 꼭 데려가라 말한 후에 방으로 돌아갔어요.

붙잡다 to grab, to hold on to | 달려들다 to throw one's self at | 서럽다 to be sad | 장모 mother-in-law | 곁 side | 달래다 to calm, to comfort | 조르다 to nag, to pester

"서방님, 어머님이 뜻밖의 이별이 답답하여 하신 말씀이니 서운해하지 마세요. 이제 곧 서방님과 이별이군요. 이 옥 반지를 가져가 저처럼 여겨 주세요."

이별할 생각을 하니 슬픈 마음에 발길이 떨어지지 않는데, 방자가 급하게 들어왔어요.

> 발(길)이 떨어지지 않다: An expression that indicates someone must leave or part but does not want to.

"도련님, 사또께서 도련님을 찾으셨어요. 잠시 친구와 인사하러 나가셨다고 둘러댔으니 어서 가세요."

방자의 말을 듣고 몽룡이 급히 떠나려는데 춘향은 몽룡의 다리를 잡고 울다가 그만 정신을 잃고 말았어요.

"향단아, 어서 찬물 떠 오너라! 늙은 어미 어쩌라고 이러느냐."

놀란 월매가 쓰러진 춘향을 일으켜 세우며 소리쳤어요.

"춘향아, 이게 웬일이냐. 나를 영원히 안 보려고 이러느냐."

몹시 괴롭고 슬픈 표정으로 몽룡이 춘향을 내려다보았어요. 춘향은 곧 기운을 차리고 일어나 말했어요.

"서방님, 한양 가는 길 편안히 가시고 종종 편지하세요."

"걱정 마라. 사람을 보내서라도 소식을 전할 테니 슬퍼하지 말고 잘 있어라. 내가 장원 급제하여 너를 꼭 데려갈 것이니 울지 말고……. 그때까지 마음 강하게 먹어야 한다."

> 장원 급제: Means to pass the state examination, taken in order to secure a government position, in first place, with the highest score.

뜻밖 unexpected | 서운하다 to be sad, to be hurt | 옥 반지 jade ring | 둘러대다 to make something up | 정신을 잃다 to lose consciousness, to faint | 쓰러지다 to collapse | 영원히 forever | 내려다보다 to look down (physically) at someone | 기운을 차리다 to perk up, to recover one's strength | 마음먹다 to make up one's mind, to have firm resolve

몽룡이 말을 타고 떠나니 춘향이 당황하며 울기 시작했어요.
춘향이 몽룡이 간 방향으로 달리며 말했어요.
"여보, 서방님, 이제 가시면 언제 오세요. 제발 연락 끊지 마세요."

당황하다 to be embarrassed, to be flustered

4
춘향, 변 사또의 수청을 거절하다

Track 04

눈물로 이별한 후, 춘향은 슬픔 속에서 세월을 보냈어요.

"향단아, 이불 깔아라. 이제 서방님을 볼 수 없으니 꿈에서라도 만나야겠구나."

"아가씨, 도련님이 장원 급제 하면 오신다 했으니 참고 기다리면 좋은 소식이 올 것입니다."

> In olden times, 아가씨 was a polite term for a young, unmarried woman.

춘향은 몽룡에 대한 걱정과 한이 가득하여 매일매일 눈물을 흘렸어요. 한양에 간 몽룡 또한 춘향이 그리워 잠을 자지 못했어요.

'보고 싶다, 보고 싶다. 밤낮 잊지 못할 내 사랑, 어서 빨리 과거 급제 해 춘향을 꼭 만나야겠다.'

몇 달 후 남원에는 변학도가 새로운 사또로 내려왔어요. 변학도는 학문도 깊고 인물도 좋았지만 지혜롭지 못하고 고집을 많이 부렸어요. 게다가 술과 여자라면 자다가도 벌떡 일어나 앉을 만큼 좋아했어요.

> 자다가도 벌떡 일어나다: Expresses that someone has such a degree of interest in something that they would even jump out of bed from their sleep for it.

이불을 깔다 to make a bed | **한** deep regret / grief | **가득하다** full | **밤낮** day and night, around the clock | **학문이 깊다** to be well-educated, to be learned | **지혜롭다** to be wise | **고집을 부리다** to be stubborn | **게다가** besides, furthermore

변 사또는 남원에 오기 전부터 춘향의 외모가 **빼어나다**는 소문을 들었어요. 그래서 '어떻게 사람들을 평안하게 보살필까?'라는 고민은 하지 않고 춘향을 볼 생각만 했어요. 남원에 들어갈 때도 백성들에게 있어 보이려고 눈에 힘을 주고, 시끄럽고 화려하게 입장했어요.

변 사또가 관청 중앙 의자에 앉자 관리들이 인사했어요.

> 눈에 힘주다: To bring force into one's eyes in order to give off an impression of strength.

그러자 변 사또가 급히 외쳤어요.

"기생들을 불러라!"

변 사또의 명령에 따라 기생들이 관청에 모였어요. 이방이 기생 이름을 하나씩 부를 때마다 아름다운 기생이 인사했지만, 변 사또의 눈에는 아무도 들어오지 않았어요. 오직 춘향이 나오기만을 기다렸어요.

> 눈에 들다: Means to take a liking to someone or something.

"여봐라, 이방. 제일 예쁘다는 춘향은 왜 없느냐?"

"춘향의 어미는 기생이나 춘향은 기생이 아니옵니다."

"기생이 아니라면 왜 그토록 이름이 유명한 것이냐?"

"기생의 딸이지만 전 사또 아들 이몽룡과 약혼을 했고, 이 도령이 과거 급제 하면 데려간다고 약속하였기에 절개를 지키며 그를 기다린다고 하여 유명합니다."

외모가 빼어나다 to be exceptionally beautiful | **평안하다** to be peaceful, to be well | **보살피다** to look after | **입장하다** to enter, to make an entrance | **관청** government office | **관리** administrator | **외치다** to shout, to yell | **이방** clerk (a government officer in the Joseon Dynasty yukbang, or six government departments, system) | **그토록** so, to such an extent | **도령** unmarried young man | **절개** chastity, faithfulness, loyalty

이방의 말을 듣고 사또는 크게 화를 내며 춘향을 당장 데리고
오라고 소리쳤어요.

"양반집 도령이 잠시 사귀었던 기생 딸을 데려가겠느냐? 다시는
그런 말 꺼내지도 말고, 춘향을 빨리 데려오거라! 만일 춘향을
데려오지 못한다면 너희들 모두에게 벌을 내릴 것이다."

변 사또의 말에 관리들이 서둘러 춘향의 집으로 뛰어갔어요.

"이리 오너라!"

놀란 춘향이 관리들의

> 이리 오너라: A word that people used in olden times to call for someone from outside the front gate of their house.

이야기를 대강 듣고 향단에게 관리들을 위해 술상을 차리라고
했어요. 춘향은 술과 안주로 정성을 다해 관리들을 대접하고 돈까지
주었어요. 그렇게 하면 돌아갈 줄 알았어요. 그렇지만 그들은
돌아가지 않았어요.

"춘향아, 너 정도의 절개는 누구나 다 가지고 있다. 너 하나 때문에
지금 관리들이 다 죽어가게 생겼으니 그만 하고 어서 가자."

춘향은 어쩔 수 없이 비틀거리며 관청으로 갔어요.

"그래요, 그럽시다. 서방님 그리워 죽으나, 새 사또에게 맞아
죽으나 죽기는 똑같으니 갑시다."

"춘향이 도착했습니다."

벌 punishment | 대강 in summary, roughly | 술상을 차리다 to set a drinking table (with food and drinks) | 안주 snacks or portions of food to be eaten while drinking | 비틀거리다 to stumble, to stagger

춘향이 사또 앞에 나와 무릎을 꿇고 앉았어요. 변 사또는 춘향의 아름다운 모습에 눈을 떼지 못하고 신이 났어요.

"춘향이 너는 오늘부터 몸단장 깨끗이 하고 나의 수청을 들어라."

> 눈을 떼지 못하다: To be so drawn (to someone or something) that you keep watching and can't look anywhere else.

"사또, 고마운 말씀이나 이미 인연을 맺은 분이 있어 그 말씀을 따르지 못하겠습니다."

"오, 얼굴만큼 마음도 아름답구나. 네가 진짜 열녀로구나. 하지만 귀한 양반 자식인 이 도령이 한때 사랑한 너를 기억이나 하겠느냐? 기다림에 지쳐 고운 얼굴에 주름이 생기고 머리도 희게 되겠구나. 차라리 나를 가까이하는 것이 어떠냐?"

> 열녀: An old word used to denote a faithful or chaste woman.

"진정한 신하는 두 임금을 따르지 않고, 열녀는 두 남편을 따르지 않는다고 했습니다. 저 또한 그렇게 할 것이니 사또의 명령을 따를 수 없습니다."

변 사또가 이 말을 듣고 크게 화를 내며 소리쳤어요.

"기생의 딸이면 너도 기생이다. 열녀는 무엇이고 절개가 무엇이냐. 사또의 명령을 따르지 않는 자는 큰 벌을 받으니 그 입 닥치지 못하겠느냐!"

> 입 닥치다: Means to close one's mouth, with the meaning here of, "Dont' speak."

무릎을 꿇다 to kneel | 신(이) 나다 to be excited | 몸단장 to dress / tidy oneself | 따르다 to obey, to follow | 한때 for a time, once | 주름이 생기다 to form wrinkles | 머리가 희다 to have grey hair | 차라리 rather, instead | 진정하다 to be true, to be genuine

"도련님에 대한 저의 깊은 마음은 변하지 않습니다. 제가 남의 첩이 되어 남편을 버리는 것은 사또께서 나라의 임금을 버리는 것과 같습니다. 그런데 어찌 남편을 버리지 않는 것이 죄가 됩니까?"

사또가 화나고 기가 막혀 책상을 탕탕 치며 소리쳤어요.

> 기(가) 막히다: Means that something is so surprising or unpleasant that it's dumbfounding.

"여봐라! 이년을 잡아다 형틀에 묶고 다리가 부서지도록 매를 쳐라."

> · 이년: A vulgar word referring to a woman.
> · V + -도록: Indicates the extent or limit of a gesture or action.

관리들이 춘향을 형틀에 묶고 매를 가져와 쳤어요. 춘향은 아픈 것을 참으려고 이를 꽉 물었어요. 이때 구경 나온 마을 사람들이 매 맞는 춘향의 모습을 보고 눈물을 흘렸어요.

"아이고! 우리 사또, 독하구나, 독해. 한양 간 남편 기다리는 춘향에게 매를 치다니?"

두 번째 매를 맞고 춘향이 말했어요.

"이 매를 맞고 죽어도 저는 도련님을 못 잊겠습니다."

세 번째 매를 맞고 춘향이 소리쳤어요.

"여자는 세 사람을 따라야 한다고 배웠습니다. 결혼하기 전에는 아버지를 따르고, 결혼한 후에는 남편을 따르고, 늙어서는 자식을 따르라기에 남편을 따른 것뿐인데 무엇이 잘못이란 말입니까?"

형틀 rack | 묶다 to tie up | 부서지다 to break | 매를 치다 to whip, to flog | 꽉 tightly, firmly | 물다 to bite | 독하다 to be cruel, to be spiteful, to be venomous

열 번을 치고도 매질이 계속되었어요. 열다섯 번째 매를 맞고, 춘향의 눈에서는 눈물이 났고 몸에서는 피가 났어요.

"달아 달아 너는 서방님이 계신 곳이 보이느냐? 나는 보이지 않는구나. 차라리 날 죽여 주시오. 죽어서 새가 된 내 울음소리를 듣고 조용한 달밤에 잠든 서방님이 깨어날 수 있게……."

춘향이 더 이상 말하지 못하고 정신을 잃자 매질하던 관리들이 눈물을 닦으며 말했어요.

"사람의 몸으로 더 이상 못 하겠네. 춘향의 절개가 정말로 대단하구나. 춘향은 하늘이 내린 열녀로구나!"

모든 사람이 눈물을 흘리자 변 사또도 마음이 좋지 않았어요.

"춘향아, 내 명령을 따르지 않으니 이렇게 고생하는 것이 아니냐? 앞으로도 계속 사또의 명령을 따르지 않을 것이냐?"

이 말에 정신을 차린 춘향이 더욱 독이 올라 말했어요.

"사또, 잘 들으십시오. 죄 없는 사람을 괴롭힌 죄를 임금님이 아시면 사또 또한 벌을 받을 것입니다. 그러니 어서 빨리 저를 죽이십시오."

"뭐야! 말이 통하지 않는구나. 여봐라! 춘향을 당장 감옥에 가둬라!"

> 말이 통하다: Means to be able to communicate or to agree with one another.

매질 whipping, flogging | **대단하다** to be incredible, to be tremendous | **고생하다** to suffer, to go through difficulties | **정신을 차리다** to gather one's wits, to return to consciousness | **독이 오르다** to become spiteful | **죄** crime, sin | **감옥** jail | **가두다** to lock up

5
춘향, 감옥에 갇히다

Track 05

춘향이 칼을 차고 나오자 월매가 정신없이 들어와 딸의 목을 안고
울었어요.

> 칼 (a cangue, or neck pillory): Indicates a rack that was used to constrain a criminal – a long and thick plank with a hole drilled into one end that went around a criminal's neck and was fastened with a large nail.

"애고, 이게 웬일이오! 내 딸이
무슨 죄를 지었기에 이렇게 칼을
차야 하오. 아이고, 기생 딸로 태어난 게 잘못이지. 춘향아, 정신
차려라. 정신 차려!"

춘향이 감옥에 들어가니 부서진 창문으로 찬바람이 들어오고
벌어진 벽 사이로 벌레가 기어 다녔어요. 월매와 향단은 집으로
돌아가고 혼자가 된 춘향은 신세가 서러워 눈물만 흘렸어요.

"내가 무슨 죄를 지었지? 나라의 쌀을 훔쳐 먹은 것도 아닌데
매를 왜 맞으며, 사람을 죽인 것도 아닌데 목에 칼은 왜 차야 하지?
억울하고 서럽구나……."

갇히다 to be locked up | 웬일 what reason | 벌어지다 to be broken, to be crumbled | 기어 다니다
to crawl around | 훔치다 to steal

춘향은 울다가 겨우 잠이 들었어요. 밤이 깊어 비가 쏟아지는데 밤에 우는 새소리가 귀신 우는 소리 같아 깜짝 놀라 눈을 떴어요. 그때 마침 감옥 밖으로 한 점쟁이가 지나가고 있었어요.

> 눈을 뜨다: Means to awaken from sleep.

지팡이를 짚고 가는 것을 보니 앞을 보지 못하는 것 같았어요.

"저기요."

"거기 누구요?"

"춘향이에요."

"춘향? 춘향이라면 남원에서 제일가는 미인 아닌가. 그런데 무슨 일로 나를 부르시는가?"

"무서운 꿈을 꿔서 꿈 풀이도 물어보고 우리 도련님이 언제 저를 찾을지 궁금하기도 해서요."

점쟁이가 그 말을 듣고 점을 쳐 주었어요.

"전라도 남원에 사는 열녀 성춘향은 언제 감옥에서 나가며, 한양 사는 이몽룡은 언제 이곳에 도착합니까?"

> 점(을) 치다: To divine the future and predict what will happen in order to judge one's fortunes and misfortunes.

점쟁이가 점을 다 치고 나서 점치는 통을 짤랑짤랑 흔들었어요.

"허허 좋다 좋아. 한양 간 서방님이 한 달 안에 내려와 평생의 한을 풀겠네."

겨우 only just, barely | **쏟아지다** to pour, to spill | **귀신** ghost, spirit | **점쟁이** fortune teller | **지팡이를 짚다** to use a cane / stick | **제일가다** to be the best | **미인** beauty | **풀이** interpretation, explanation | **통** container

그 말을 들은 춘향의 목소리가 조금 밝아졌어요.

"그렇게 되면 얼마나 좋겠어요."

"아니, 그렇게 될 것이니 조금만 참으시오."

점쟁이가 이리 말을 하고 있는데 어디선가 까마귀가 날아와 까옥까옥 하고 울었어요. 느낌이 좋지 않아 춘향이가 손을 휘휘 저으며 까마귀를 날려 보냈어요.

> 까옥까옥: Expresses the ceaseless sound of a crow's cry.

"까마귀야, 네가 나를 잡으려고 온 것이구나!"

"아니! 까마귀가 우는 것은 평생의 한을 풀 일이 생긴다는 뜻이니 너무 걱정하지 말게."

그제야 춘향은 한숨을 쉬며 걱정을 덜었어요.

까마귀 crow | 휘휘 swish, whoosh | 젓다 to wave, to shake | 걱정을 덜다 to assuage concerns, to lessen worries

6

몽룡, 암행어사가 되다

Track 06

한편 한양에 올라간 몽룡은 밤낮으로 글공부에만 힘썼어요.
처음에는 춘향이 그리워 아무것도 하지 않고 방에서 잠만 잤어요.
하지만 춘향이 꿈에 나타나 걱정하는 것을 보고 마음을 다잡았어요.

마침 나라에 좋은 일이 있어
과거 시험을 치른다는 소식이

> 마음(을) 잡다/다잡다: Means to collect oneself and settle one's excited or troubled feelings.

들려왔어요. 몽룡이 책을 들고 과거 시험장에 들어가니 전국에서
똑똑하다는 사람들은 모두 모여 있었어요. 다행히 몽룡이 잘 아는
문제가 나와 뛰어난 글씨체와 내용으로 제일 먼저 답을 써냈어요.

몽룡은 자신의 소원대로 장원 급제 하였고 전라도 암행어사가

되었어요.

> N + 대로: Indicates that something is based on or grounded in the preceding word.

> During the Joseon Dynasty, 암행어사 (amhaengeosa, a secret royal inspector) was a temporarily held government position that entrusted the holder with the job of receiving a special mission from the king. These inspectors were given a 마패, a badge that allowed them to borrow local government horses as they traveled the country.

글공부 study, reading and writing | 힘쓰다 to work hard, to make an effort | 시험을 치르다 to hold an exam, to take / sit an exam | 전국 the whole country | 다행히 luckily, fortunately | 뛰어나다 to be outstanding, to be excellent | 글씨체 penmanship, calligraphy | 소원 wish, hope

임금께서 주신 마패를 받고 나오는 몽룡의 모습은 깊은 산속의
호랑이와 같았어요.

집에 돌아와 부모님께 인사드린 후 몽룡은 떠날 준비를 했어요.
몽룡은 어사라는 것을 숨기기 위해 가난한 사람의 옷을 입었어요.
한눈에 봐도 거지 같았어요. 거기에 낡은 가방을 메고 그 가방 안에
마패를 숨겼어요.

> 한눈: Means a single glance or to look for a short
> time. Here, it means that even looking once
> would be enough to know he was a beggar.

몽룡은 여유 있게 남원을 향해 내려갔어요. 빨리 춘향을 보고
싶었지만, 어사로서 사람들이 어떻게 살고 있고 어떻게 생각하고
있는지 알아보는 일도 중요했기 때문에 일하는 농부들의 노래나
대화에도 귀를 기울였어요.

> 귀(를) 기울이다: Means for someone to focus their
> attention on and listen thoughtfully and carefully
> to another person's speech or opinion.

몽룡이 남원 근처에
이르렀을 때, 농부 한 명이
담배를 피우며 잠깐 쉬고 있었어요. 몽룡이 농부에게 물었어요.

"춘향이가 새로 온 사또의 수청을 들어 뇌물을 많이 받고 사람들을
괴롭힌다는 말이 사실인가?"

농부가 화를 내며 몽룡에게 물었어요.

"어디에서 살다가 왔소?"

"내가 어디에서 왔든 무슨 상관인가?"

숨기다 to hide, to conceal | 가난하다 to be poor | 낡다 to be worn, to be shabby | 여유 있다 to be
relaxed | 농부 farmer | 이르다 to reach, to arrive at | 뇌물 bribe | 괴롭히다 to torment, to bother
| 상관 correlation

"무슨 상관? 거기는 눈도 없고 귀도 없나? 지금 춘향이가 수청을 들지 않겠다고 해서 매를 맞고 갇혀 있는데, 무슨 소리를 하는 거야! 거지 주제에 춘향이 이름을 더럽히다가는 굶어 죽기 십상이지. 한양 간 이 도령인지 삼 도령인지, 그 자식은 올라간 후 소식을 뚝 끊었다지. 사람이 그 모양이니 무슨 벼슬을 하겠어!"

> • V/A + −기 십상이다: Used to indicate that the situation in the preceding clause can easily or is very likely to occur.
> • 이 도령인지 삼 도령인지: Wordplay making use of the fact that Master Lee's family name is pronounced the same as the number two.

몽룡은 농부와 대화를 끝내고 쓸쓸하게 돌아섰어요. 그때 마침 아이 하나가 혼잣말을 하며 걸어오고 있었어요.

"오늘이 며칠이지? 한양까지 며칠이나 걸릴까? 불쌍한 춘향이는 옥에 갇혀 어떻게 됐을까? 이 도령은 왜 연락도 하지 않지? 양반들은 어쩌면 그리 냉정할까?"

"아이야, 넌 어디서 왔니?"

"남원에서요."

"어디 가니?"

"한양에요."

"무슨 일로 가니?"

"춘향이 편지 갖고 이몽룡 집에요."

"잠시 그 편지 좀 보자."

이름을 더럽히다 to damage / bring down someone's honor or dignity | 굶다 to starve | 쓸쓸하다 to be forlorn, to be dismal | 혼잣말 talking to oneself | 냉정하다 to be cold-hearted

"왜 남의 부인의 편지를 보자고 하십니까?"

"내가 도움을 줄 수도 있지 않니? 본다고 없어지는 것도 아니니
한번 보자꾸나."

몽룡의 말이 맞는 것도 같아 아이는 편지를 주었어요. 몽룡이
편지를 급하게 열어 보니 춘향의 글씨체가 분명했어요. 감옥에서
편지를 쓸 도구를 구할 수 없으니 손가락을 깨물어 피로 쓴
글이었어요.

도구 tool, implement | 구하다 to find, to obtain | 깨물다 to bite

이별 후에 오래도록 소식이 끊겼군요. 서방님은 부모님 모시고 편안하신지요? 저는 새로 오신 사또의 수청을 거절했다가 감옥에 갇혀 있습니다. 언제 죽을지 몰라 서방님께 편지로 이별을 전합니다.

춘향의 편지를 보고 몽룡은 자기도 모르게 눈물이 떨어졌어요. 그 모습을 본 아이가 이상하게 생각되어 편지를 달라고 했어요.

"이 도령은 내 친구다. 내일 남원에서 만나기로 약속했으니 너도 같이 가자."

"싫어요. 편지 주세요."

아이가 몽룡의 옷을 잡고 밀다가 몽룡의 가방에서 마패가 떨어졌어요.

"이놈! 만일 마패를 보았다고 말하면 살아남지 못할 것이다."

몽룡은 아이에게 비밀을 지킬 것을 약속받고 남원으로 갔어요.

살아남다 to survive

7

몽룡, 거지가 되어 나타나다

Track 07

해가 질 무렵, 몽룡은 춘향의 집에 도착했어요. 몽룡이 춘향의
집에 들어가니 월매가 물을 떠 놓고 하늘에 빌고 있었어요.

"하느님, 하느님, 하나밖에
없는 제 딸, 춘향을 살려

> Water represents clarity and cleanliness. This passage
> is about praying one's wish will come true while
> offering up the purest and cleanest water to god.

주십시오. 저희를 불쌍히 여기시고, 한양 간 이몽룡이 과거에
급제하게 해 주세요."

월매가 기도하는 모습을 본 몽룡은 코끝이 찡했어요.

'내가 장원 급제한 것이 조상 덕인 줄 알았는데 알고 보니 우리
장모 덕이로구나!'

"안에 누구 있느냐?"

몽룡은 큰 소리로 외치며 안으로 들어갔어요.

"누구요?"

"나요."

"나라니, 누구신가?"

"이 서방이요."

> 서방: A word affixed to a
> family name that is used to
> designate a son-in-law, a
> younger brother-in-law, etc.

무렵 around, at about the time of | 하느님 god | 코끝이 찡하다 to be choked up | 덕 thanks,
by virtue of

"이 서방이라니. 아, 저 건넛마을 이 씨 아들 이서방?"

"어허, 장모. 사위 목소리도 잊었나?"

"누구? 아이고! 이 사람, 어디 갔다 이제 왔소? 춘향이 소식 듣고 살리러 왔소? 어서어서 들어가오."

월매는 놀란 목소리로 말했어요. 그런데 촛불을 앞에 두고 몽룡을 자세히 살펴보니 거지 중에 상거지 모습이었어요.

"아니, 왜 이 모양인가?" 상거지: Means a very miserable, dreadful, and pitiful beggar.

"장모, 양반이 한번 잘못되니 말로 할 수가 없네. 한양에 갔더니 벼슬길은 막히고 재산도 다 없어졌더라고. 춘향에게 내려와 돈 좀 얻어 갈까 하고 왔더니 여기도 말이 아닐세."

이 말을 들은 월매는 기가 막혀 말이 안 나왔어요. 너무 화가 나 몽룡의 코를 잡아 비틀었어요.

이다/아니다 + -ㄹ세: Low speech used to indicate that the speaker is explaining their thoughts to the listener.

"이 냉정한 사람아! 이별 후 소식 하나 없어도 꼭 데리러 오겠다는 약속만 믿고 과거 급제하기만 기다린 우리 춘향이를 어찌 살려 낼 텐가!"

"장모, 나 배고파 죽겠네. 밥 좀 먼저 주시오."

"뭐? 뭐라? 자네 줄 밥 없네."

건넛마을 neighboring village | 벼슬길 path into government service | 재산 fortune, property, assets | 비틀다 to twist

이때 감옥에서 춘향을 만나고 돌아온 향단이 몽룡의 목소리를
듣고 방 안으로 뛰어 들어와 인사했어요.

"도련님, 향단이 인사드립니다. 먼 길 평안히 다녀오셨습니까?"

향단은 춘향 아가씨가 그토록 그리워하던 몽룡을 보니 반가워
눈물을 줄줄 흘렸어요. 그러고는 부엌으로 들어가 남은 밥에
간장과 김치를 놓고, 냉수 가득 떠서 상을 차려 왔어요. 몽룡은 밥과
반찬을 한꺼번에 붓더니 정신없이 먹었어요. 이때 향단은 아가씨를
생각하여 크게 울지도 못하고 눈물을 삼켰어요.

> 눈물을 삼키다: Expresses forcefully holding back tears or cries, etc.

"향단아, 울지 마라. 춘향이가 설마 죽기야
하겠느냐? 지은 죄가 없으면 반드시 나올 것이다."

몽룡은 감옥에서 고생하고 있을 춘향을 생각하니 마음이
아팠어요.

"향단아, 이제 상 치워라. 장모, 춘향이나 보러 갑시다."

마침 새벽을 알리는 종소리가 들려왔어요. 몽룡은 향단의 뒤를
따라 감옥 앞에 도착했어요.

"춘향아!"

몽룡의 목소리가 들리자 춘향이 깜짝 놀라 잠에서 깼어요.

"이게……. 꿈인가? 서방님 목소리가 들리네."

그토록 so much, to such an extent | **간장** soy sauce | **냉수** cold water | **한꺼번에** all together,
all at once | **붓다** to pour | **설마** surely, truly, never | **상(을) 치우다** to clear the table

몽룡이 좀 더 큰 소리로 춘향을 불렀어요.

"춘향아, 정신 차리고 나를 보거라. 내가 왔다."

"오다니, 누가 와요?"

월매가 짜증스러운 말투로 춘향에게 말했어요.

"너의 서방인지는 잘 모르겠는데, 거지는 분명하다."

춘향이 몽룡에게 다가와 창살 사이로 몽룡의 손을 잡고 숨이 막혀 한동안 말없이 울기만 했어요. 춘향이 정신을 차려 자세히 보니 몽룡의 모습이 불쌍하기 짝이 없었어요.

> A + -기(가) 짝(이) 없다: Indicates that something is so incredible or terrible that there is nothing to which it can be compared.

말투 one's manner of speaking | 창살 bars in a window | 숨이 막히다 to be unable to breathe, to stifle

"서방님, 제 몸 하나 죽는 것은 서럽지 않으나 서방님은 어쩌다 이 모양이 되었습니까?"

"괜찮다, 춘향아. 걱정하지 마라. 사람 목숨은 하늘에 달렸는데 설마 죽기야 하겠느냐?"

> 사람 목숨은 하늘에 달렸다: Means that how long or short a person's life will be is out of their control.

이 말을 듣고 춘향이 어머니를 불렀어요.

"어머니, 공든 탑이 무너졌네요. 제 신세가 불쌍하게 되었지만 저 죽은 후에도 서방님을 미워하지 마세요. 제가 입던 비단옷을 팔아 서방님의 옷을 사 드리세요.

> 공든 탑이 무너지랴: (proverb) (literally, "A tower built through hard work will not collapse.") A saying that means that what is done with all one's heart will not be in vain. Here, Chunhyang is using it comparatively to say that all her efforts have led instead to a poor result.

은비녀와 반지도 팔아 갓과 신발을 사 주세요. 제가 없어도 서방님을 잘 보살펴 주세요."

이번에는 몽룡의 손을 잡고 부탁했어요.

"서방님, 내일은 변 사또의 생일입니다. 생일잔치에 저를 불러 또 매를 칠 것입니다. 여기서 더 맞으면 저는 살 수가 없습니다. 제가 죽으면 서방님이 직접 저를 묻어 주세요. 그리고 제가 죽으면 불쌍하신 우리 어머니에게는 피붙이가 아무도 없습니다. 제 어머니를 춘향이처럼 생각하고 보살펴 주시면 죽어서도 은혜를 갚겠습니다."

은비녀 silver hairpin | 갓 gat (traditional Korean hat worn by men) | 묻다 to bury | 피붙이 blood relative

춘향은 말을 마치고 서럽게 울었어요.

"울지 마라, 춘향아. 하늘이 무너져도 솟아날 구멍은 있다고 했다.
나만 믿고 기다려 보아라."

몽룡은 자신이 어사가 되었다고
밝히고 싶었지만 그럴 수 없었어요.

> 하늘이 무너져도 솟아날 구멍은 있다: (proverb)
> (literally, "Even if the sky should fall,
> there's a hole through which to escape.")
> A saying that means that no matter how
> difficult the circumstances one faces, a
> way to survive will always appear.

말도 못 하고 춘향을 보고만 있자니 답답해서 견딜 수가 없었어요.
몽룡은 우는 춘향을 달래고 월매와 향단을 집으로 돌려보낸 후
광한루에 올라갔어요. 몽룡의 뒤에는 어사를 수행하는 관리들이
조용히 뒤따르고 있었어요.

"내일은 사또의 생일잔치 날이다. 분위기가 최고에 달할 때 내가
신분을 밝힐 것이니 너희들도 사람들 눈에 띄지 않게 기다리고
있어라."

밝히다 to reveal | **견디다** to bear, to endure | **돌려보내다** to send back, to return | **수행하다** to
attend to someone, to follow someone of rank in fulfilling their duty | **뒤따르다** to follow, to go after |
달하다 to reach, to come to | **신분** status, position, rank | **눈에 띄다** to draw attention

8
암행어사 출두야!

Track 08

다음 날 이웃 마을의 관리들이 변 사또의 생일을 축하하기 위해 남원으로 몰려들었어요. 잔치에는 여러 가지 과일들과 귀한 술, 음식이 놓여 있었고 한쪽에는 음악에 맞춰 기생들이 춤을 추고 있었어요. 문밖에서 지켜보던 몽룡은 당장 들어가 모두 벌하고 싶었지만, 화를 참고 안으로 어슬렁어슬렁 걸어 들어갔어요.

"여봐라. 좋은 잔치에 술과 안주 좀 얻어먹고 가자."

이미 변 사또가 거지들의 출입을 금지했기 때문에 포졸들은 몽룡이 들어오는 것을 막았어요. 그때 운봉 지방의 사또가 몽룡을 보고 변 사또에게 부탁했어요.

"저 거지가 비록 옷은 대단하지 않지만 양반인 것 같으니 맨 끝자리에 앉히고 술이나 먹여 보냅시다."

변 사또가 인심 쓰듯 허락하자 몽룡이 운봉의 곁에 앉았어요. 이때 다른 손님들 앞에는 여러 가지 술과 안주가 차려져 있는데 자신의 상에는 막걸리 한 잔이 전부였어요.

> 운봉 (Unbong): Used here to call the magistrate from that region by the region's name.

몰려들다 to flock, to descend on, to swarm | **어슬렁어슬렁** leisurely | **얻어먹다** to be treated to food, to beg for food | **포졸** constable, soldier who worked for the government in the Joseon era | **막다** to stop, to block | **인심(을) 쓰다** to be kind, to be generous | **막걸리** makgeolli, rice wine

몽룡은 자신의 상을 발길로 탁 차며 운봉 상에 놓인 갈비를 잡았어요.

"갈비 좀 먹읍시다."

몽룡이 쩝쩝 소리를 내며 점잖지 않게 갈비를 먹어 치우고 있는데 운봉이 변 사또에게 말했어요.

"사또, 즐거운 잔치에 시가 없어서 되겠습니까? 운을 넣어 시를 지어 봅시다."

> 운: Means to write a poem with a character with the same sound in the same place in each line. At the time, noblemen showed off their skills to write verses that rhymed certain Chinese characters.

"그거 좋습니다, 운봉. 어떤 글자를 넣어 지을까요?"

"사또, 높다는 의미의 고와 기름을 뜻하는 고, 두 글자를 넣어서 지어 봅시다."

이때 듣고 있던 몽룡이 일어나서 말했어요.

"나도 부모 덕에 어려서부터 책을 좀 읽었습니다. 이렇게 좋은 잔치에 대접만 받고 그냥 가기 미안하니 제가 한번 지어 보겠습니다."

다른 사람들이 시를 다 짓기도 전에 몽룡이 몇 자 쓰더니 금방 자리에서 일어났어요.

발길 a foot extended sharply forward | **갈비** galbi, beef ribs | **점잖다** to be polite, to be refined |
시를 짓다 to write a poem

금 그릇의 맛있는 술은 백성의 피요,
옥쟁반에 좋은 안주는 백성의 기름이라.
촛농 떨어질 때 백성의 눈물이 떨어지고
노랫소리 높아질 때 백성의 울음소리 높아 간다.

변 사또는 술에 취해 몽룡의 시가 무슨 뜻인지 몰랐지만 운봉은 가슴이 철렁 내려앉았어요.

> 가슴이 내려앉다: To be surprised or to feel drained from receiving a large shock

'아이쿠! 큰일이 났구나!'

운봉이 서둘러 일어나 신발도 제대로 신지 못하고 나갔어요.

"운봉, 어디 가십니까?"

"잠시 화장실에 다녀오겠습니다."

큰일이 났다는 것을 알고 몇몇 관리들이 슬금슬금 자리를 뜨는데 변 사또는 눈치 없이 춘향을 데려오라고 명령했어요.

> 자리를 뜨다: Means to leave a place in order to go to another.

이때 몽룡이 눈짓하자, 그를 따르는 포졸들이 마패를 들고 큰소리로 외쳤어요.

> 눈짓하다: Means to move one's eyes to signal something or give instructions to another.

"암행어사 출두야!"

금 그릇 golden dishes | 백성 the common people | 옥쟁반 jade dishes | 촛농 candle drippings |
술에 취하다 to be drunk | 큰일 trouble, serious issue | 몇몇 several, some | 눈치 one's awareness,
one's senses

그 순간 즐거웠던 잔치판의 분위기가 바뀌었어요. 변 사또
밑에서 일하는 사람들이 당황하는 사이에 다른 마을의 관리들은
도망가기 바빴어요. 변 사또는 벌벌 떨다가 숨을 곳을 찾아 도망가기
시작했어요. 이를 본 포졸들이 달려들어 변 사또를 잡았어요.

"애고, 나 죽네!"

이때 어사 옷을 입고 나타난 몽룡이 큰 소리로 말했어요.

"변 사또를 당장 감옥에 가둬라."

그리고 감옥에 갇힌 죄인들의 죄를 물은 뒤 죄 없는 사람들은 풀어
주기로 했어요.

도망가다 to flee, to run away | 벌벌 떨다 to shake, to tremble | 숨다 to hide

9

춘향과 몽룡, 사랑을 이루다

Track 09

드디어 춘향의 차례가 되어 몽룡은 죄를 물었어요.

"저 여인의 죄는 무엇이냐?"

관리가 춘향의 죄를 말했어요.

"기생 월매의 딸인데 사또의 수청을 거절한 죄로 감옥에 갇혔습니다."

"어미가 기생이면 그 딸도 기생이 분명하다. 기생이면 사또의 수청을 드는 게 당연한데 수청을 거절하고 어찌 살기를 바라느냐? 죽어 마땅하지만 내 수청을 받아 주면 목숨은 살려 주겠다."

몽룡이 춘향의 마음을 떠보려고 나무라니 춘향은 기가 막히고 어이가 없었어요.

> 어이없다: Means to experience something so sudden that one is dumbfounded. ⓢⓨⓝ 어처구니없다

"내려오는 사또마다 모두가 똑같구나! 어사는 들으십시오. 푸른 소나무가 눈이 온다고 색이 변하겠습니까? 제 마음은 변할 리 없으니 빨리 죽여 주십시오."

> Even if white snow gathers on a green pine tree, the tree doesn't change its green color. Through this meaning, this expression compares Chunhyang's faithfulness to the pine tree.

> V/A + -(으)ㄹ 리(가) 없다: Used to indicate a person's certainty that there is no chance of the contents in the preceding clause ever happening.

당연하다 to be natural, to be reasonable | 마땅하다 to be appropriate, to be suitable, to be right | 마음을 떠보다 to feel out what is in someone's heart, to get a read on someone's feelings | 나무라다 to scold, to rebuke | 소나무 pine tree

몽룡은 더 참을 수 없어, 주머니에서 옥 반지를 꺼내어 관리에게
주었어요.

"이것을 춘향에게 주어라."

춘향이 반지를 받아 보니, 몽룡과 이별할 때 자신이 준
옥 반지였어요. 깜짝 놀란 춘향에게 몽룡이 말했어요.

"춘향은 얼굴을 들어 나를 보아라."

춘향이 고개를 들어 보니 거지의 모습으로 찾아왔던 서방님이
어사또로 앉아 있었어요.

"나를 알아보겠느냐? 네가 기다리던 서방이 바로 나다. 춘향아."

어사또 inspector

춘향은 잠시 이것이 꿈은 아닌지 고민했어요. 정신을 차리고 몽룡을 바라보는 춘향의 눈에서 구슬 같은 눈물이 떨어졌어요. 몽룡은 춘향에게 다가가 꼭 안아 주었어요. 그 모습을 본 월매와 향단은 기뻐하며 덩실덩실 춤을 추었고 구경 왔던 마을 사람들도 자기 일처럼 모두 기뻐하였어요.

춘향 모녀를 집으로 돌려보낸 후 몽룡은 밤늦도록 관청의 일을 살피고 새벽이 되어서야 춘향을 찾아갔어요. 춘향은 몽룡의 얼굴을 만져 보고 손을 잡더니 한참을 울었어요.

"그만 울어라. 어려움 끝에 행복이 있다고 하지 않더냐? 앞으로 우리가 이별하는 일은 없을 것이니 울지 마라. 처음 약속대로 오래오래 같이 살자꾸나."

춘향과 몽룡은 날 밝을 때까지 서로의 얼굴을 바라보며 그동안 못 한 이야기를 나누었어요.

다음 날 몽룡은 춘향 모녀와 향단을 데리고 한양으로 향했어요. 많은 사람이 입에 침이 마르도록 칭찬했어요.

그 후, 임금은 목숨 걸고 정절을 지킨 춘향을 칭찬하여 정렬부인이라는 이름을 내렸어요. 그리고 몽룡은 여러 벼슬을 다 지내고 벼슬에서 물러난 이후에도 춘향과 아들 딸 낳고 오래오래 행복하게 잘 살았어요.

> 침이 마르다: Means to speak repeatedly about someone or something.

> • 정렬부인: In the Joseon Dynasty, a title given to a proper and chaste woman.
> • 내리다: For a person of higher standing to hand down an award or punishment to a person of lower standing, or to inform them of orders, instructions, etc.

구슬 bead, marble | 덩실덩실 dancing joyfully | 밤늦다 to be late at night | 살피다 to survey, to check over | 향하다 to face, to head | 목숨(을) 걸다 to risk one's life | 정절 chastity, loyalty | 정렬부인 "Lady of Virtue" | 물러나다 to retire, to step back

부록
Appendix

1

1 **'-는 바람에'를 사용하여 부정적인 결과에 대한 원인을 나타내는 문장을 만드세요.**
Use -는 바람에 to make sentences that show the cause of a negative consequence.

(1) 갑자기 비가 오다   •   •   ① 출근 시간에 늦었어요.

(2) 휴대 전화를 잃어버리다   •   •   ② 등산을 하지 못했어요.

(3) 버스를 잘못 타다   •   •   ③ 잠을 못 잤어요.

(4) 급하게 먹다   •   •   ④ 전화를 할 수 없었어요.

(5) 옆집에서 떠들다   •   •   ⑤ 체해서 병원에 갔어요.

(1) _____

(2) _____

(3) _____

(4) _____

(5) _____

2 빈칸에 알맞은 단어를 넣어 문장을 완성하세요.

Put the correct word in each blank to complete the sentences.

| 그네 | 근심 | 허락 | 글재주 |

(1) 월매는 결혼 후 계속 자식이 없어 ( )로/으로 병을 얻게 되었다.

(2) 춘향은 어릴 때부터 책을 좋아해서 ( )이/가 뛰어났다.

(3) 몽룡은 아버지께 외출 ( )을/를 받았다.

(4) 춘향은 예쁘게 단장하고 ( )을/를 타러 집을 나섰다.

3 이야기의 내용과 맞으면 ○, 틀리면 × 표시하세요.

Mark ○ if the statement is true, and mark × if it is false.

(1) 춘향은 전라도 남원에 살았다. ( )

(2) '몽룡'은 용처럼 귀하게 자라라는 뜻이다. ( )

(3) 몽룡은 춘향의 소문을 듣고 광한루로 갔다. ( )

(4) 몽룡은 춘향이 기생의 딸이기 때문에 불렀다. ( )

(5) 춘향은 결혼하자는 몽룡의 말을 듣고 처음에는 거절했다. ( )

4 한국에는 여러 명절이 있어요. 그중 여자는 그네를 타고 남자는 씨름을 하며, 하루를 보내는 명절은 무엇인가요?

Korea has many holidays. Which of the following holidays is a day that women spend riding swings and men spend wrestling?

① 설 ② 추석

③ 단오 ④ 동지

5 **다음 질문에 알맞은 답을 쓰세요.**
Write the correct answer for each of the following questions.

(1) 월매가 간절하게 자식을 갖고 싶어 하는 이유는 무엇인가요?

_____

_____

(2) 몽룡이 방자를 시켜 춘향을 부를 때 춘향은 어떤 말로 거절했나요?

_____

_____

(3) 몽룡은 춘향의 거절을 듣고 어떤 말을 다시 전했나요?

_____

_____

2

1 **빈칸에 알맞은 단어를 넣어 문장을 완성하세요.**
Put the correct word in each blank to complete the sentences.

세월	권하다	드나들다	승낙하다

(1) 몽룡이 찾아오자 월매는 방으로 모신 후 차와 담배를 (   ).

(2) 월매는 몽룡의 말을 듣고 춘향과의 결혼을 (   ).

(3) 부부의 인연을 맺은 후 몽룡은 춘향의 집을 자주 (   ).

(4) 사랑에 빠진 춘향과 몽룡은 (   ) 가는 줄 몰랐다.

2 상황에 알맞은 표현을 찾아 연결하세요.

Connect each situation with the appropriate expression.

(1) 몽룡이 춘향을 보고 싶어
해가 지기만을 기다릴 때 　　　•

•　① 한 입으로 두말하지 않는다

(2) 몽룡이 월매가 자신의 말을
믿게 하고 싶을 때 　　　•

•　② 목이 빠지게 기다린다

3 다음 사람들은 서로를 어떻게 부르나요? 빈칸에 알맞은 것을 쓰세요.

How do the following people address one another? Fill in the blanks with the correct words.

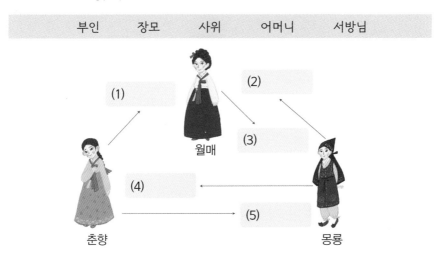

| 부인 | 장모 | 사위 | 어머니 | 서방님 |

4 다음 대화에 공통으로 들어갈 말로 알맞은 것을 고르세요.

Choose the correct word that can be used in both of these dialogues.

> **A** 월 매: 그사이 평안하셨는지요?
> 　몽 룡: (　　)이/가 춘향이 모친인가?
> **B** 학 생: 선생님, 방학 동안 잘 지내셨습니까?
> 　선생님: 그래, (　　)도 잘 지냈나?

① 너　　　　　　② 당신　　　　　　③ 그대　　　　　　④ 자네

5 다음 질문에 알맞은 답을 쓰세요.
Write the correct answer for each of the following questions.

(1) 월매가 위와 같이 말한 진짜 이유는 무엇인가요?

도련님, 순간의 감정으로 결혼한다고 하시는데,
그런 말씀 마시고 그냥 차 한잔하시고 가십시오.

_____

(2) 몽룡은 이 말을 하기 전 춘향에게 어떤 노래를 불러 주었나요?

얘, 춘향아. 우리 업기 놀이나 하자.
이리 와 업히어라.

_____

3

1 빈칸에 알맞은 단어를 넣어 대화를 완성하세요.
Put the correct word in each blank to complete the dialogues.

승진	이별	종종	차리다	처리하다

(1) A 루이 씨, 같이 갈까요?

   B 어쩌죠? 저는 아직 (   ) 일이 남았어요.

(2) A 고향에 계신 부모님이 보고 싶어요.

   B 저도 그럴 땐 (   ) 영상 통화를 해요.

(3) A 감기에 걸려 일을 할 수 없네요.

   B 저런, 빨리 병원 가서 치료받고, 기운 (   ).

(4) A 현지 씨, (   ) 축하해요.

    B 감사해요. 다 여러분들이 도와주었기 때문이에요.

(5) A 후이 씨는 언제 가장 슬펐어요?

    B 가족과 (   )하고 한국에 올 때가 가장 슬펐어요.

2 빈칸에 알맞은 단어를 넣어 문장을 완성하세요.

Put the correct word in each blank to complete the sentences.

터지다	쓰러지다	달려들다	고백하다

(1) 몽룡은 춘향과의 일을 어머니께 (   ).

(2) 어머니의 꾸중을 들은 몽룡은 춘향을 보자마자 울음이 (   ).

(3) 갑자기 이별 소식을 들은 월매는 몽룡에게 (   ).

(4) 몽룡이 떠나려 하자 춘향은 울다가 (   ).

3 각 인물들의 속마음으로 알맞은 것을 골라 연결하세요.

Connect each of the characters with their true feelings.

(1)   •

                      • ① '떠난다는 말을 어떻게 꺼낼지 걱정이네?'

(2)    •

                      • ② '너무 조르면 곤란해하시겠지?'

(3)   •

                      • ③ '처음부터 결혼을 허락하는 것이 아니었어.'

4 다음 질문에 알맞은 답을 쓰세요.

Write the correct answer for each of the following questions.

(1) 몽룡의 어머니는 무슨 말로 몽룡을 나무랐나요?

_____

_____

(2) 춘향이는 몽룡을 보내며 마지막으로 어떤 부탁을 했나요?

_____

_____

4

1 다음 문장에 어울리는 단어를 찾아 ○ 표시하세요.

Circle the word that best suits each of the following sentences.

(1) 한양에 간 몽룡이 그리워 춘향은 잠을 (안, 못) 이루었다.

(2) 춘향은 한양으로 떠난 몽룡에 대한 걱정이 (그리워, 가득하여) 매일매일 눈물을
   흘렸다.

(3) 변 사또는 지혜롭지 못하고 고집을 부렸다. (그러나, 게다가) 술과 여자를 좋아했다.

(4) 춘향은 자신 때문에 관리들이 다칠까 봐 (거절, 친절)하지 못했다.

(5) 춘향이 자신의 말을 듣지 않자 변 사또는 춘향의 다리가 (부서지도록, 무너지도록)
   매를 치라고 명령했다.

(6) 춘향이 끝내 마음을 바꾸지 않자 변 사또는 춘향에게 (칼, 줄)을/를 씌워 감옥에
   가두라고 했다.

2 다음 문장에 공통으로 들어가는 신체 부위로 알맞은 것을 고르세요.

Choose the body part that correctly fits in all of the following sentences.

> A. 변 사또는 (　　　)에 힘을 주며 시끄럽고 화려하게 남원에 입장했다.
>
> B. 아무리 예쁜 기생들이 들어와도 변 사또의 (　　　)에 드는 사람은 없었다.
>
> C. 드디어 춘향이 나오자 변 사또는 춘향에게서 (　　　)을 떼지 못했다.

① 눈　　　　　　　② 코　　　　　　　③ 입　　　　　　　④ 귀

3 이야기의 내용과 맞으면 ○, 틀리면 × 표시하세요.

Mark ○ if the statement is true, and mark × if it is false.

(1) 춘향은 이 도령이 너무 보고 싶어 꿈에라도 만나기를 소원했다.　　　(　　　)

(2) 몽룡은 과거 급제 전에 춘향을 보러 갈 결심을 했다.　　　(　　　)

(3) 변 사또는 춘향이 몽룡과 결혼을 약속한 것을 모르고 춘향을 불렀다. (　　　)

(4) 춘향이 매를 맞다 기절하자 변 사또와 관리들은 눈물을 흘렸다.　　　(　　　)

4 '열녀'는 한 사람을 향한 마음이 변하지 않는 것을 말합니다. 다음 중 열녀와 관계있는 것을 모두 고르세요.

열녀 (a virtuous woman) refers to someone whose feelings for another person are unwavering. Choose all of the following that are related to 열녀.

① 한　　　　　　　② 절개　　　　　　　③ 인연　　　　　　　④ 정절

5 **다음 질문에 알맞은 답을 쓰세요.**
Write the correct answer for each of the following questions.

(1) 춘향이 변 사또의 수청을 들 수 없는 이유가 무엇인가요?

_____

_____

(2) 춘향의 말을 들은 변 사또는 어떤 말로 춘향의 마음을 바꾸려 하였나요?

_____

_____

(3) 춘향이 변 사또를 향해 마지막으로 한 말은 무엇인가요?

_____

_____

5

1 **빈칸에 알맞은 단어를 넣어 대화를 완성하세요.**
Put the correct word in each blank to complete the dialogues.

갇히다	쏟아지다	억울하다	벌어지다

(1) A 커피가 (   ) 옷에 얼룩이 생겼어요.

   B 세탁소에 맡겨 보면 어때요?

(2) A 상처가 (   ) 안 되니까 무리한 운동은 하지 마세요.

   B 네, 알겠습니다.

(3) A 어제 엘리베이터가 고장 나서 10분이나 (   ).

    B 뭐? 정말 무서웠겠다.

(4) A 죄 없는 사람이 10년이나 감옥에 있었대요.

    B 그 사람은 정말 (   ).

2 빈칸에 알맞은 단어를 넣어 문장을 완성하세요.
Put the correct word in each blank to complete the sentences.

겨우	귀신	덜다	밝아지다

(1) 점쟁이가 하는 말을 듣고 춘향의 목소리가 (   ).

(2) 춘향은 감옥에서 울다가 (   ) 잠이 들었다.

(3) 춘향은 새소리가 (   ) 우는 소리 같아 잠에서 깼다.

(4) 춘향은 점쟁이가 몽룡이 한 달 안에 돌아온다는 말을 듣고 걱정을 (   ).

3 어울리는 것끼리 연결하여 문장을 완성하세요.
Connect the phrases that go together to create complete sentences.

(1) 사람을 죽인 것도 아닌데   •   • ① 조금만 참으시오.

(2) 밤에 우는 새소리에   •   • ② 목에 칼은 왜 씌우나?

(3) 곧 몽룡이 올 것이니   •   • ③ 놀라 잠을 깼다.

4 다음 그림을 보고 각각의 모습을 묘사해 보세요.

Look at and describe each of the following images.

(1) 감옥의 모습은 어떠한가요?

_____

_____

_____

_____

_____

_____

(2) 점쟁이의 모습은 어떠한가요?

_____

_____

_____

_____

_____

_____

5 다음 질문에 알맞은 답을 쓰세요.
Write the correct answer for each of the following questions.

(1) 춘향이 점쟁이를 부른 까닭은 무엇인가요?

_____

_____

(2) 점쟁이는 까마귀가 우는 것을 보고 어떻게 풀이했나요?

_____

_____

6

1 아래의 단어와 '-기 십상이다'를 사용하여 문장을 완성하세요.
Choose the best word for each blank and then add -기 십상이다 to create a complete sentence.

| 후회하다 | 미끄러지다 | 식물이 죽다 |
| 사고가 나다 | 건강이 나빠지다 | |

(1) 겨울철에 집에만 있으면 _____.

(2) 운전 중에 휴대 전화를 보면 _____.

(3) 물과 햇볕이 없는 곳에서는 _____.

(4) 건강 관리를 안 하면 나중에 _____.

(5) 눈길에서 자전거를 타다가는 _____.

2 이야기의 내용과 맞으면 ○, 틀리면 × 표시하세요.

Mark ○ if the statement is true, and mark × if it is false.

(1) 한양에 올라간 몽룡은 처음부터 열심히 글공부를 했다. ( )

(2) 몽룡이 관리로 일할 장소로 전라도를 택한 것은 춘향을 보기 위해서이다. ( )

(3) 몽룡은 춘향이 수청을 거절해 옥에 갇혔다는 소식을 농부에게 들었다. ( )

(4) 춘향은 피로 편지를 써서 자신의 상황을 몽룡에게 전하려 했다. ( )

(5) 편지를 전하던 아이는 처음부터 몽룡이 암행어사임을 알았다. ( )

3 어울리는 것끼리 연결하여 문장을 완성하세요.

Connect the phrases that go together to create complete sentences.

(1) 몽룡이 가난한 사람의   •   • ① 한눈에 봐도 거지 같았다.
    옷을 입으니

(2) 몽룡은 백성의 마음을   •   • ② 몽룡은 가슴이 철렁
    읽기 위해   내려앉았다.

(3) 춘향의 이름을 더럽히는 •   • ③ 농부의 말에 귀를 기울였다.
    몽룡에게

(4) 춘향이 갇혔다는   •   • ④ 농부는 화를 내었다.
    사실을 알고

4 춘향이 감옥에서 손가락을 깨물어 피로 편지를 쓴 이유는 무엇인가요?

For what reason does Chunhyang bite her finger in jail and use her blood to write a letter?

① 몽룡의 눈에 잘 띄게 하려고

② 글을 쓸 먹을 구할 수 없어서

③ 자신의 절개를 보여 주기 위해서

④ 옥중에서 손가락을 깨물다 피가 나서

5 **다음 질문에 알맞은 답을 쓰세요.**

Write the correct answer for each of the following questions.

(1) 한양에 간 몽룡이 공부를 열심히 하게 된 이유는 무엇인가요?

_____

_____

(2) 몽룡은 아이가 가지고 있는 편지를 보려고 어떤 말을 했나요?

_____

_____

7

1 **빈칸에 알맞은 단어를 넣어 대화를 완성하세요.**

Put the correct word in each blank to complete the dialogues.

무렵	재산	밝히다	치우다	수행하다

(1) A 여기 있는 물건들 좀 (　　　　　) 도와줄 수 있어요?

　　B 그럼요. 도와줄게요.

(2) A 우리 내일 저녁에 그 맛집에 한번 가 볼까요?

　　B 네, 그런데 좀 일찍 출발해야 해요. 5시 (　　　　　)부터 기다리는 줄이 길더라고요.

(3) A 대통령 곁에는 (　　　　　) 사람들이 항상 따라다녀요.

　　B 당연하죠. 한 나라를 대표하는 중요한 인물이니까요.

(4) A 어제 떡볶이 가게 할머니에 대한 뉴스 봤어요?

   B 30년 동안 모은 전 ( )을/를 기부하신 할머니 뉴스 말이지요?
   네, 봤어요. 정말 대단하세요.

(5) A 얼마 전 있었던 오토바이 사고 기억하지요? 그 사고의 원인이 ( )?

   B 아니요, 얼른 원인이 나와야 할 텐데 걱정이에요.

2 빈칸에 알맞은 표현을 넣어 문장을 완성하세요.

Put the correct expression in each blank to complete the sentences.

> 코끝이 찡하다   눈에 띄다   눈물을 삼키다
> 기가 막히다   불쌍하기 짝이 없다

(1) 월매가 기도하는 모습을 본 몽룡은 ( ).

(2) 사또가 화나고 ( ) 책상을 탕탕 치며 소리쳤어요.

(3) 이때 향단이는 아가씨를 생각하여 크게 울지도 못하고 ( ).

(4) 춘향이 정신을 차려 자세히 보니 몽룡의 모습이 ( ).

(5) "분위기가 최고에 달할 때 내가 신분을 밝힐 것이니 너희들도 사람들 ( )
   않게 기다리고 있어라."

3 다음 중 춘향이 몽룡에게 한 말을 고르세요.

Choose which of the following Chunhyang said to Mongryong.

① 배고파 죽겠으니
밥 좀 주세요.

② 제가 죽으면 직접 저를
묻어 주세요.

③ 하늘이 무너져도 솟아날
구멍은 있습니다.

④ 제가 입던 비단옷과 은비녀,
반지를 팔아 주세요.

4 **빈칸에 알맞은 단어를 넣어 대화를 완성하세요.**

Put the correct word in each blank to complete the dialogue.

마침	설마	더욱	보면

몽룡: 장모, 사람 목숨은 하늘에 달렸다는데 (1) (　　　　　　　　) 춘향이 죽겠소?

월매: 거지 차림에 말도 잘하는구려. 그러니 내가 (2) (　　　　　　　　) 화가 나오.

향단: 도련님, (3) (　　　　　　) 새벽을 알리는 종이 울리니 춘향 아씨를 뵈러
　　　 가시지요.

몽룡: 그래, 가자. 춘향이 나를 (4) (　　　　　　) 기뻐할 것이다.

5 **다음 질문에 알맞은 답을 쓰세요.**

Write the correct answer for each of the following questions.

(1) 정화수를 놓고 비는 월매를 본 몽룡은 어떤 생각을 했나요?

_____

_____

(2) 춘향이 몽룡을 보고 '공든 탑이 무너졌네.'라고 말한 까닭은 무엇인가요?

_____

_____

8

1 **빈칸에 알맞은 단어를 넣어 문장을 완성하세요.**
Put the correct word in each blank to complete the sentences.

막다	몰려들다	슬금슬금	인심 쓰다	시를 짓다

(1) 변 사또의 생일을 축하하는 수령들이 남원으로 (   ).

(2) 포졸들은 몽룡이 잔치하는 곳에 들어오는 것을 (   ).

(3) 변 사또는 (   ) 몽룡이 음식을 먹는 것을 허락했다.

(4) 음식을 배불리 먹은 대가로 몽룡은 (   ).

(5) 몽룡이 암행어사라는 것을 눈치챈 운봉은 (   ) 일어나 도망쳤다.

2 **이야기의 내용과 맞으면 ○, 틀리면 × 표시하세요.**
Mark ○ if the statement is true, and mark × if it is false.

(1) 변 사또는 생일잔치에 거지들을 들어오지 못하게 명령했다.   (   )

(2) 운봉은 몽룡이 어사임을 알고 잔치에 참석하도록 부탁했다.   (   )

(3) 몽룡을 포함해 잔치에 참석한 모든 사람 앞에 갈비가 놓였다.   (   )

(4) 변 사또는 술에 취해 몽룡이 지은 시를 이해하지 못했다.   (   )

(5) 변 사또는 암행어사 출두 소리를 듣고 화장실에 갔다.   (   )

(6) 몽룡은 변 사또를 감옥에 가두었다.   (   )

3 어울리는 것끼리 연결하여 문장을 완성하세요.
Connect the phrases that go together to create complete sentences.

(1) 비록 옷은 대단하지 않지만 •

(2) 변 사또가 인심 쓰듯 허락하자 •

(3) "암행어사 출두야!" •

• ① 그 순간 즐거웠던 잔치판의 분위기가 바뀌었어요.

• ② 몽룡이 운봉의 곁에 앉았어요.

• ③ 양반인 것 같으니 술이나 먹여 보냅시다.

4 다음 중 이몽룡의 시에 들어갈 말로 알맞은 것을 고르세요.
Choose the correct words that belong in Lee Mongryong's poem.

금 그릇의 맛있는 술은 백성의 (㉮)요
옥쟁반에 좋은 안주는 백성의 (㉯)이라.
촛농 떨어질 때 백성의 (㉰)이 떨어지고
노랫소리 높아질 때 백성의 (㉱)이 높아 간다.

(㉮)	(㉯)	(㉰)	(㉱)
① 울음소리	눈물	기름	피
② 기름	피	울음소리	눈물
③ 피	기름	눈물	울음소리
④ 눈물	울음소리	피	기름

5 **다음 질문에 알맞은 답을 쓰세요.**
Write the correct answer for each of the following questions.

(1) 운봉은 변 사또에게 무엇을 하자고 제안했나요?

_____

_____

_____

(2) 몽룡이 암행어사 출두를 한 후 한 일은 무엇인가요? 두 가지를 적으세요.

① _____

② _____

9

1 **아래의 단어와 '-(으)ㄹ 리가 없다'를 사용하여 문장을 완성하세요.**
Choose the best word for each blank and then add -(으)ㄹ 리가 없다 to create a complete sentence.

> 성적이 좋다   쉽게 무너지다   일을 대충하다
> 장사가 잘 되다   결과가 좋지 않다

(1) 수업 시간에 졸면 _____.

(2) 그 사람은 꼼꼼해서 _____.

(3) 그 건물은 튼튼하기 때문에 _____.

(4) 지금까지 열심히 노력했는데 _____.

(5) 좋은 재료를 사용하지 않으면 _____.

2 빈칸에 알맞은 단어를 넣어 문장을 완성하세요.

Put the correct word in each blank to complete the sentences.

침	옥 반지	살피다	마땅하다

(1) 몽룡은 처음에 춘향에게 사또의 수청을 들지 않았기 때문에 죽어 (　　　　　)
말했다.

(2) 춘향은 (　　　　　)을/를 보고 암행어사가 몽룡이라는 것을 알았다.

(3) 몽룡은 밤늦도록 관청의 일을 (　　　　　) 새벽이 되어서야 춘향을 찾아갔다.

(4) 많은 사람들이 약속을 지킨 몽룡과 춘향을 보고 입에 (　　　　　)이/가
마르도록 칭찬했다.

3 다음 중 춘향이 암행어사에게 자신의 절개(변하지 않는 마음)를 나타내기 위해 인용한
것은 무엇인가요?

Which of the following does Chunhyang use to express her faithfulness (her unwavering heart) to
the secret royal inspector?

① 옥 반지　　　　　　　　　　② 푸른 소나무

③ 비단 주머니　　　　　　　　　④ 기생의 신분

4 다음 질문에 알맞은 답을 쓰세요.

Write the correct answer for each of the following questions.

(1) 암행어사 몽룡은 춘향의 마음을 떠보려고 어떤 말을 했나요?

_____

_____

(2) 춘향을 만난 몽룡은 왜 춘향과 같이 집으로 돌아가지 않았나요?

_____

_____

<u>1 ~ 9</u>

1 다음 그림을 참고하여 '춘향전'의 줄거리를 써 보세요.

Use the following image to write a short summary of "The Story of Chunhyang."

2 여러분이 만약 춘향 또는 몽룡이었다면 연인과 신분 차이가 나는 상황에서 어떻게
할 건가요?

If you were Chunhyang or Mongryong, what would you do in a situation in which you loved
someone from a different social standing?

(1) 춘향이었다면, _____

_____

(2) 몽룡이었다면, _____

_____

3 '춘향전'과 같이 여러분 나라에도 신분 차이를 이겨낸 사랑 이야기가 있나요?
소개해 봅시다.

Is there a story from your country like "The Story of Chunhyang," where love overcomes
differences in social standing? Introduce it here.

_____

_____

_____

_____

_____

_____

_____

1장

1 (1) ② 갑자기 비가 오는 바람에 등산을 하지
못했어요.

(2) ④ 휴대 전화를 잃어버리는 바람에 전화를
할 수 없었어요.

(3) ① 버스를 잘못 타는 바람에 출근 시간에
늦었어요.

(4) ⑤ 급하게 먹는 바람에 체해서 병원에
갔어요.

(5) ③ 옆집에서 떠드는 바람에 잠을 못 잤어요.

2 (1) 근심 　　　　(2) 글재주

(3) 허락 　　　　(4) 그네

3 (1) ○ 　　(2) × 　　(3) ×

(4) × 　　(5) ○

4 ③

5 (1) 조상 무덤에 향은 누가 피우며 죽은 뒤 제사
는 누가 치를까 걱정이 됐다.

(2) 내가 비록 기생 딸이지만 여염집 여자이기
때문에 부른다고 함부로 갈 수 없다.

(3) 춘향을 기생으로 여기는 것이 아니라 글을
잘한다기에 부르는 것이다.

2장

1 (1) 권했다 　　　　(2) 승낙했다

(3) 드나들었다 　　(4) 세월

2 (1) ② 　　　　　　(2) ①

3 (1) 어머니 　　　　(2) 장모

(3) 사위 　　　　(4) 부인

(5) 서방님

4 ④

5 (1) 몽룡의 진심을 알고 싶었다.

(2) 이리 오너라 업고 놀자.
사랑 사랑 내 사랑이야.
사랑이로구나, 내 사랑 사랑이야.

3장

1 (1) 처리할 　　　　(2) 종종

(3) 차리세요 　　　(4) 승진

(5) 이별

2 (1) 고백했다 　　　(2) 터졌다

(3) 달려들었다 　　(4) 쓰러졌다

3 (1) ② 　　(2) ① 　　(3) ③

4 (1) 양반의 자식이 부친을 따라 지방에 왔다 첩
을 얻어 가면 앞길이 막히고 벼슬을 못 하게
된다.

(2) 한양 길 편히 가시고 종종 편지해 달라고 부
탁했다(부디 소식을 끊지 말라는 부탁).

4장

1 (1) 못 　　　　　　(2) 가득하여

(3) 게다가 　　　　(4) 거절

(5) 부서지도록 　　(6) 칼

2 ①

3 (1) ○ 　　(2) × 　　(3) × 　　(4) ×

4 ②, ④

5 (1) 이미 인연을 맺은 분이 있어서 수청을 들 수
없다.

(2) 귀한 양반 자식인 이 도령이 한때 사랑한 춘
향을 기억할 리 없으니 차라리 자신을 가까이
하는 것이 낫다.

(3) "사또, 잘 들으십시오. 죄 없는 사람을 괴롭힌
죄를 임금님이 아시면 사또 또한 벌을 받을
것입니다. 그러니 어서 빨리 저를 죽이십시
오."

5장

1 (1) 쏟아져서 　　　(2) 벌어지면

(3) 갇혀있었어 　　(4) 억울했겠어요

2 (1) 밝아졌다 　　　(2) 겨우

(3) 귀신 　　　　(4) 덜었다

3 (1) ②　　(2) ③　　(3) ①

4 (1) 감옥의 창문이 부서져 있다. 부서진 창문으로 찬바람이 들어오고 있다. 벽이 벌어져 있고 벌레가 기어 다닌다.

(2) 점쟁이는 지팡이를 짚고 있고 앞을 보지 못한다. 지팡이를 짚지 않은 손에는 점치는 통을 들고 있다.

5 (1) 무서운 꿈을 꿔서 꿈풀이도 물어보고 이몽룡이 언제 춘향을 찾을지 궁금하기도 했다.

(2) 평생의 한을 풀 일이 생긴다.

6장

1 (1) 건강이 나빠지기 십상이다
(2) 사고가 나기 십상이다
(3) 식물이 죽기 십상이다
(4) 후회하기 십상이다
(5) 미끄러지기 십상이다

2 (1) ×　　(2) ×　　(3) ○
(4) ○　　(5) ×

3 (1) ①　　(2) ③　　(3) ④　　(4) ②

4 ②

5 (1) 춘향이 꿈에 나타나 걱정하는 것을 보았다.
(2) "내가 도움을 줄 수도 있지 않니? 본다고 없어지는 것도 아니니 한번 보자꾸나."

7장

1 (1) 치우려고 하는데　　(2) 무렵
(3) 수행하는　　(4) 재산
(5) 밝혀졌나요

2 (1) 코끝이 찡했어요
(2) 기가 막혀
(3) 눈물을 삼켰어요
(4) 불쌍하기 짝이 없었어요
(5) 눈에 띄지

3 ②

4 (1) 설마　　(2) 더욱　　(3) 마침　　(4) 보면

5 (1) 자신이 장원 급제 한 것이 조상의 덕인 줄 알았는데 알고 보니 장모의 덕이었다는 생각을 했다.

(2) 몽룡이 과거 급제 하기를 정성을 다해 빌었는데 거지가 되어 나타났기 때문이다.

8장

1 (1) 몰려들었다　　(2) 막았다
(3) 인심 쓰듯　　(4) 시를 지었다
(5) 슬금슬금

2 (1) ○　　(2) ×　　(3) ×
(4) ○　　(5) ×　　(6) ○

3 (1) ③　　(2) ②　　(3) ①

4 ③

5 (1) 즐거운 잔치에 시가 없어서는 안 되니 운을 넣어 시를 지어 보자고 제안했다.
(2) ① 변 사또를 감옥에 가두었다.
② 감옥에 갇힌 죄인들의 죄를 물은 뒤 죄 없는 자는 풀어 주었다.

9장

1 (1) 성적이 좋을 리가 없다
(2) 일을 대충할 리가 없다
(3) 쉽게 무너질 리가 없다
(4) 결과가 좋지 않을 리가 없다
(5) 장사가 잘 될 리가 없다

2 (1) 마땅하다고　　(2) 옥 반지
(3) 살피다가　　(4) 침

3 ②

4 (1) "어미가 기생이면 그 딸도 기생이 분명하다.
기생이면 사또의 수청을 드는 게 당연한데
수청을 거절하고 어찌 살기를 바라느냐? 죽
어 마땅하지만 내 수청을 들면 목숨은 살려
주겠다."

(2) 암행어사의 책임을 다하기 위해서(관청의 일
을 살피기 위해서) 돌아가지 않았다.

1~9장

1 몽룡은 단옷날 그네를 타는 춘향이를 보고 첫눈
에 반했다. 몽룡은 춘향의 집에 가서 결혼을 승
낙 받고 두 사람은 행복한 시간을 보냈다. 하지
만 몽룡은 공부하러 한양으로 떠나 춘향과 헤어
지게 되었다. 그사이 새로 온 변 사또가 춘향에
게 수청을 들라고 했고 춘향은 이를 거절하여
감옥에 갇히게 되었다. 한편 한양에 간 몽룡은
장원 급제 하여 남원으로 내려왔다. 자신의 신
분을 숨기고 옥에 갇힌 춘향을 찾아 온 후 변 사
또의 생일날 자신의 신분을 밝혔다. 몽룡은 나쁜
변 사또를 벌하고 남원의 사또가 되어 춘향과
다시 만나 행복하게 살았다.

1

Lee Mongryong and Seong Chunhyang meet at Gwanghallu Pavilion

p. 11

During the Joseon dynasty, there lived in the city of Namwon in Jeolla-do Province a gisaeng named Wolmae. Wolmae had been a famous gisaeng in her youth, but married Vice Minister Seong, a nobleman, and became his concubine. However, after her marriage, she still bore no children, and eventually fell sick from worry.

Wolmae spoke to Vice Minister Seong.

"I don't know what good favor I received in my previous life to have come to be together with you, my lord. But I, who have no parents or siblings – if I have no child, who will burn incense at the grave of my ancestors, and who will perform the memorial rites after I die? If I go pray at a famous temple and beget a child, I think the greatest regret of my life will be resolved."

p.12

From that day forward, Vice Minister Seong and his wife traveled around the most renowned mountains in the country and prayed and prayed to the spirits for 100 days.

"Spirits, please let us have a child."

As if in answer to their devoted prayers, 10 months later, Wolmae gave birth to a beautiful daughter. Wolmae called her Chunhyang, meaning "fragrance of spring," and looked after her like a precious jewel. From the time she was young, Chunhyang liked books and had a talent for writing, and she grew to be more and more well-mannered and beautiful. And so in Namwon, there was no one who didn't know of Chunhyang.

Meanwhile, in Hanyang, there lived a nobleman named Lee Hanrim. He came from a renowned family who had been government officials since the time of their ancestors, and he had a son. His son's name was Lee Mongryong, "mong" meaning "dream" and "ryong" meaning "dragon," because Lee Hanrim's wife had dreamt of a dragon before Mongryong was born. Mongryong was 16 years old, obeyed to his parents, and also had a talent for writing.

p.13

One day, Mongryong called to his servant, Bangja.

"Bangja, where in Namwon is there a spot with a good view?"

"Why is my master, who is studying, looking for a spot with a good view?"

"You say that because you don't know what you're talking about. Since the olden days, haven't the greatest scholars gone to a place with a good view to take in the sights while studying? Besides, today is Dano, isn't it? Don't scold me, recommend a place, quickly."

Banja introduced places in Namwon with a good view to Mongryong.

"For a view in Namwon, if you head to the east, Seonwonsa Temple is good; to the west, there's Gwanwangmyo Shrine; to the south, there's Ojakgyo Bridge at Gwanghallu Pavilion, and Yeongjugak Pavilion; and to the north, there's Gyoryongsanseong Fortress. You can decide where you'd like to go, Master."

"Hm, let's go to Ojakgyo Bridge at

Gwanghallu Pavilion."
Mongryong first got permission from his father to go out, and then called for Bangja and told him to prepare a donkey. They went to see the sights, with Bangja leading the donkey on which Mongryong rode. When they approached Gwanghallu Pavilion, Mongryong came down off the donkey and climbed up the pavilion. He looked around and the view was very good.

p.14

On Dano, Chunhyang also got made up prettily and put on a silk skirt to go with Hyangdan to Gwanghallu Pavilion to ride the swings. With just her white socks on her feet, stomping down on a swing tied high in a willow tree, Chunhyang's appearance was that of a beautiful fairy descending on a cloud.
"Bangja, what's that going back and forth between the branches of the willow tree over there? Go take a close look and come back."

p.16

At Mongryong's word, Bangja went to examine what the master had seen across the pavilion, and then came back.
"It's Chunhyang, the daughter of a gisaeng from this village named Wolmae. Though her mother is a gisaeng, Chunhyang is proud and won't be one herself. She has learned all the manners that a woman should have, and is even talented at writing, no different from a young maiden from a decent family."
Mongryong, who was curious about Chunhyang, called to Bangja to bring her over.
"Over here, Chunhyang!"
"Why are you shouting so loudly and frightening me!"
By calling out so loudly, Bangja startled Chunhyang.
"Hey, something's happened. Something's happened. My master, the son of the magistrate, came to Gwanghallu Pavilion and saw you riding that swing, and is calling for you to come over."
"How does your master know me to call me over? You've been babbling on like a chatty lark, haven't you!"

"No, no. This is your fault. If a girl like yourself is going to ride a swing, she should do so quietly in her own home.

How can she do so at Gwanghallu Pavilion, where so many people are gathered? The master saw that and fell in love at first sight, so let's hurry and go over to him."

p.17

"Today's Dano, isn't it? The girls from other families are all riding swings. And another thing, I might be the daughter of a gisaeng, but I'm a girl of a decent home, and to recklessly call me over...... I can't go."

When Bangja passed these words on to Mongryong, Mongryong's heart was drawn even further toward Chunhyang.

"My master says, 'I'm not thinking of Chunhyang as a gisaeng; I'm calling her over because of her talent for writing. It may be unusual to call over a girl from a decent home, but don't think of it as something wrong and come over for a moment, would you?'"

Chunhyang heard this and, pretending as if she had no choice, followed Bangja to Gwanghallu Pavilion where Mongryong was. Chunhyang stepped lightly up the pavilion and greeted Mongryong. Seeing Chunhyang sitting up properly with her lovely air, Mongryong had this thought:

"It's as if a fairy came down from heaven to the earth in Namwon! Chunhyang's face and her manner don't belong to a person of this world!"

Chunhyang looked Mongryong over as well, and saw that his good looks were exceptional. The space between his two eyebrows was high, like a person whose name would be well-known, and his forehead, nose, chin, and cheekbones all went together nicely, giving him the look of someone who would become a great person. Looking at Mongryong, Chunhyang fell in love at first sight and shyly lowered her head.

p.18

"What's your family name and how old are you?"

"My family name is Seong and I'm 16 years old."

"Oho, you're the same age as I am! Your family name is different from mine, so this is clearly a match made in heaven. Are both your parents alive?"

"Only my mother, and I'm her only child."

"An only daughter, are you? Chunhyang, we met like this because heaven has decided our fate, so let's live together forever."

"We've met for the first time today, so how can you say that this is fate? You're the son of a nobleman, my lord, and I'm the child of a lowly concubine; how will I live on if, after I give my heart to you, you abandon me? Don't say such things, please."

"Don't speak like that. I'm going to marry you and we'll be a couple. I'll go to your house tonight, so I'd be glad if you'd welcome me in kindly."

2

Mongryong and Chunhyang promise to wed

p.19

After Mongryong had left Chunhyang and returned home, he opened a book, but he thought only of Chunhyang and nothing of the book would stay in his mind. He waited eagerly for the sun to set. As soon as the day turned dark, Mongryong leapt up.

"Bangja! Lead me to Chunhyang's house, quickly."

Mongryong followed Bangja and arrived at Chunhyang's house. Bangja went beneath the window of Chunhyang's room and called to her. Surprised, Chunhyang woke her mother in the opposite room.

"Mother, Bangja has brought his master." Hearing this, Wolmae called for Hyangdan.

"Hyangdan! Clear the room and light some candles."

Wolmae, who rushed out of the room, was over 50 years old, but her appearance was tidy and as beautiful as ever. Chunhyang's beauty was the result of her resembling her mother.

p.20

Wolmae gathered her hands together and greeted Mongryong politely.

"My lord, are you well?"

"Are you Chunhyang's mother? Have you been well, too?"

"Yes. I'm not sure how we can properly welcome you, my lord, in gracing our home." Wolmae brought Mongryong inside and, after offering him tea and tobacco, called for Chunhyang. Chunhyang quietly entered the room and stood there shyly.

"Today, I saw Chunhyang by chance at Gwanghallu Pavilion and fell in love with her at first sight, so I've come here like this, like the butterfly seeks out the flower. I want to marry Chunhyang; what do you think?"

"My lord, when I was young, the gentleman Vice Minister Seong briefly came down to Namwon from Hanyang. I couldn't disobey his order to serve to him as his mistress, and so I did. Then just three months later, he left for Hanyang, and afterwards, I had my daughter, Chunhyang. But the vice minister left this world without ever being able to see Chunhyang's face, and I've been raising her on my own until now.

p.21

But even though she's a child from a house of high rank, I was lacking, and unable to send her to be married before she turned 16. My lord, you speak of getting married out of the feelings you've felt for an instant, but don't say such things; simply drink your tea and go on your way."

In order to determine Mongryong's sincerity, what Wolmae spoke was different from how she truly felt.

"Wolmae, though I can't hold a big wedding with my parents in attendance, do you think the child of a nobleman would speak falsely to you? I'll treat Chunhyang as my first wife, so please, don't worry and give me your permission."

Wolmae considered for a moment and then happily consented.

"Our Chunhyang is paired with Master Lee now. And I'll think of you as my son-in-law, my lord. Hyangdan, set a table with drinks and snacks, quickly."

Chunhyang poured a cup full to the brim with liquor and gave it to Mongryong, and then Mongryong placed it in front of him and spoke.

"I'm sorry that I can't hold a proper wedding for you. Chunhyang, take this liquor as the promise of our marriage and let's drink up."

p.22

Once they were married, Mongryong frequented Chunhyang's house often, as if it were his own. Chunhyang, who at first had been shy and simply blushed, began to show her smile. Mongryong couldn't hold back his overflowing love and sang a song.

Come here, let me carry you on my back and play, love, love, my love.
You are my love, aren't you, my love.

"Hey, Chunhyang. Let's play at piggyback. Come here and let me carry you."
Chunhyang stood still for a moment, shy, and then pretended as if she had no choice and let herself be carried.
"Wow, you're very heavy, aren't you! How does it feel to be carried on my back?"
"It's so very nice."
Time passed quickly as the two of them sang and played at carrying one another and being carried. When the two 16-year-olds met, they knew nothing of time passing them by.

3
Chunhyang and Mongryong bid farewell

p.24

A year passed. Chunhyang and Mongryong were still deeply in love and were playing on the day when Bangja quickly rushed over.
"Master! Master! The magistrate is calling for you."
Mongryong hurried home and found that orders had come down to the magistrate from Hanyang.
"Mongryong, the king has told me to go to Hanyang to work in a higher position within the government. I'll take care of a few remaining things before I go, so you take your mother and leave for Hanyang tomorrow."
Mongryong was happy for the news of his father's promotion, but when he thought about parting with Chunhyang, all his strength left his arms and legs, and he grew agitated and wept.
"What's this? Why are you crying? Did you think you'd live in Namwon for the rest of your life? We're going to Hanyang for something good, so don't think of this with disappointment and go get ready to leave."

p.25

After listening to his father, Mongryong went inside and confessed his relationship with Chunhyang to his mother. But he simply ended up being scolded by her at length. On the way to Chunhyang's house to tell her what had happened, Mongryong tried his best to hold back his tears. And then, upon seeing her, he could hold it no longer and burst out crying. Chunhyang was surprised and asked,

"My husband, what is it? Don't cry. Tell me what's the reason for this."

"My father has been promoted and is going to Hanyang."

"Really? That's good news, then, so why are you crying?"

"Because we'll have to part... I didn't have the heart to tell my father, so instead, I told my mother and then she was furious. She asked who would look on me favorably, the son of a nobleman who followed his father to the countryside and took a concubine before a wife. There would be no way forward and I might not be able to become a government official, so there's no choice for me now except to part with you."

Once she heard Mongryong explain the situation, Chunhyang grew angry. And then she felt how unfair her life was and began to cry.

"It's no use. I didn't even know that we could be parted this easily, but I gave you all of my heart just the same. Oh, my wretched life."

Wolmae heard the sound of Chunhyang crying and thought the two of them might be having a lover's quarrel, so she listened outside the door for a while, but was surprised that it was not a lover's quarrel at all, but talk of parting.

p.26

She opened the door immediately and rushed into the room.

"Oh, my neighbors! Today, two people will die in this house."

As Wolmae shouted, she grabbed onto Chunhyang.

"Chunhyang, let's die together. Let's die,

quickly now, so that at the very least, the master can take our bodies with him."

Wolmae struck her chest and threw herself at Mongryong.

"Tell me what crime has my daughter Chunhyang committed that you're leaving her behind... Is Chunhyang lacking in some way? Should Chunhyang die from missing you, my lord, on whom shall I depend to survive? Oh, how sorrowful, oh, how terrible!"

"Mother, don't be so sad. If I come back to take Chunhyang with me later, it'll all be fine."

Chunhyang, who had been watching Mongryong from aside, comforted Wolmae.

"Mother, don't pester my husband too much. It seems that perhaps we'll have no choice but to part at this time. Please, ask him to be sure to come back later to take me with him once he's made his way in Hanyang."

Wolmae listened to Chunhyang and, after asking Mongryong to be sure to come take Chunhyang with him, went back to her room.

p.27

"My husband, my mother said those things because this farewell is unexpected and distressing, so don't feel too hurt. We'll have to be parted soon now, won't we? Take this jade ring and consider it as you would me."

Thinking of parting made him sad and he felt reluctant to leave, but Bangja rushed in.

"Master, the magistrate was looking for you. I thought something up and told him you went out to say a short goodbye to a friend, so we should leave quickly."

Mongryong made to leave in a hurry after hearing Bangja's words, but Chunhyang grabbed hold of his leg and cried, and in the end, she passed out.

"Hyangdan, bring cold water, quickly! How

can you do this to your old mother?"
Startled, Wolmae stood the collapsed
Chunhyang upright and shouted.
"Chunhyang, what's happened to you? Will
you leave me alone forever like this?"
Mongryong looked down at Chunhyang
with an incredibly hurt and sad expression.
Chunhyang soon recovered her strength,
rose, and spoke.
"My husband, have a safe journey to
Hanyang and write me often."
"Don't worry. Even if I have to send someone,
you'll have news of me, so don't be sad, and
stay well. When I win first place in the state
examination, I'll definitely come back for you,
so don't cry... Until then, your resolve must
be strong."

p.28

When Mongryong rode off on his horse,
Chunhyang grew flustered and began to cry.
She ran in the direction in which Mongryong
had gone and spoke.
"Darling, my husband. If you go now, please
come back someday. Please don't fall out of
touch."

4

Chunhyang refuses to serve Magistrate Byeon

p.29

After their tearful parting, Chunhyang passed
the time in sadness.
"Hyangdan, make the bed. I can't see my
husband now, so I should at least meet him
in my dreams."
"Miss, the young master said he'd win first
place in the state examination and come
back, so if you hold on and wait, good news
will come."
Chunhyang cried every day, full of worry and
grief for Mongryong. And Mongryong, who
had gone to Hanyang, couldn't sleep for
missing Chunhyang.
*"I miss you, I miss you. My love, whom I can't
forget day or night; I must hurry and pass the
state examination and meet Chunhyang."*
Some months later, Byeon Hakdo, a new
magistrate, arrived in Namwon. Byeon Hakdo
was well-educated and attractive, but he
was unwise and extremely stubborn. What's
more, he would sit up out of sleep with a
jump when it came to alcohol and women, he
enjoyed them so.

p.30

From even before Magistrate Byeon had
come to Namwon, he had heard rumors of
Chunhyang's remarkable beauty. And so he
thought nothing of, "How shall I look after
the people in my charge well?" but only of
seeing Chunhyang. And when he arrived in
Namwon, to show off to the peasants, he
steeled his gaze and made a loud and flashy

entrance. Magistrate Byeon sat in a chair at the center of the government office and the administrators greeted him. And then he quickly shouted.

"Bring in the gisaengs!"

At Magistrate Byeon's order, the gisaengs gathered at the government office. As a clerk called their names out one by one, each beautiful gisaeng greeted Magistrate Byeon, but none of them caught his eye. He waited only for Chunhyang to appear.

"See here, clerk. Why is Chunhyang, the most beautiful of them all, not here?"

"Chunhyang's mother is a gisaeng, but Chunhyang is not."

"If she isn't a gisaeng, why is her name so well-known?"

"Though she's the daughter of a gisaeng, she was betrothed to Lee Mongryong, the son of the previous magistrate, and he's promised to pass the state examination and come back for her; she is well-known for remaining faithful as she waits for him."

p.31

The magistrate heard the officer speak and grew furious, and shouted for Chunhyang to be brought over immediately.

"The son of a nobleman is going to come back for the daughter of a gisaeng whom he was with only briefly? Don't ever say something like that again. Hurry and fetch Chunhyang! If you can't fetch her, you'll all be punished."

At Magistrate Byeon's word, the administrators all ran in a rush to Chunhyang's house.

"Come out!"

A surprised Chunhyang listened to the gist of what the administrators said, and

then told Hyangdan to set a drinking table for them. She put her all into greeting the administrators, treating them to drinks and morsels of food, and even gave them money. She thought if she did so, they would leave. But they did not.

"Listen, Chunhyang, anyone else is just as faithful as you are. But just because of you alone, all of the administrators are going to die, so stop it and let's go now, quickly."

With no other choice, Chunhyang staggered along to the government office.

"All right, let's do as you say. Whether I die from longing for my husband or die at the hands of the new magistrate, I'll die anyway, so let's go."

"Chunhyang has arrived."

p.32

Chunhyang appeared in front of the magistrate and kneeled. Magistrate Byeon was excited and couldn't take his eyes off of Chunhyang's beautiful appearance.

"Chunhyang, from today on, get yourself dressed nice and cleanly, and come and serve me as my mistress."

"Magistrate, your words are kind, but there is another to whom I am already tied, so I cannot do as you say."

"Oh, your heart is as lovely as your face. You're truly a virtuous woman, aren't you? But do you think Master Lee, the precious son of a nobleman, will remember you, whom he loved once? You'll grow tired of waiting and your beautiful face will grow wrinkled and your hair will go grey. Why not come closer to me instead?"

"It has been said that a true subject does not obey two kings, and a virtuous wife does not obey two husbands. And I will do the same,

so I cannot follow your orders."
Hearing this, Magistrate Byeon grew very angry and shouted.
"If you're the daughter of a gisaeng, then you're a gisaeng, too. What's this about a virtuous woman? What's this about being faithful? Those who don't follow my orders as a magistrate are punished harshly, so can't you shut that mouth of yours?"

p.33

"My true feelings for my lord will not change. For me to become the concubine of another and abandon my husband would be the same as for you, Magistrate, to abandon your king. So then how can it be a crime for me to not abandon my husband?"
The magistrate was angry and dumbfounded, and he pounded on his desk and shouted.
"See here! Seize this wench and tie her to the rack, and whip her until her legs break."
The administrators tied Chunhyang to the rack and brought out a whip and lashed her. Chunhyang bit down firmly with her teeth to endure the pain. At that moment, villagers who emerged to see what was happening saw Chunhyang being whipped and they shed tears.
"Oh! Our magistrate is a cruel one, so cruel. Chunhyang, who's waiting for her husband who left for Hanyang – he's having her whipped?"
Chunhyang was whipped a second time, and spoke.
"Even if I'm whipped to death, I cannot forget my lord."
She was whipped a third time and cried out.
"I was taught that a woman should obey three people. Before marriage, she should obey her father; after marriage, she should

obey her husband; and when she grows old, she should obey her children. And so I'm simply following my husband, so what can you say I've done wrong?"

p.34

Even after ten lashes, the whipping continued. Chunhyang was lashed 15 times, and tears leaked from her eyes and her body was bloodied.
"Oh moon, oh moon, do you see where my husband is? I can't see it after all. Better to kill me instead. I'll die and become a bird, so that my cries can wake my husband from his sleep on a quiet, moonlit night…"
Chunhyang couldn't speak any longer and lost consciousness, and the administrators who had whipped her spoke while wiping tears from their eyes.
"As a person, I can stand this no more. Chunhyang's loyalty is truly incredible. She's

a virtuous woman who descended from heaven, after all!"

Once everyone began to cry, Magistrate Byeon grew unsettled.

"Chunhyang, aren't you suffering because you won't obey my command? Will you go on refusing to obey your magistrate's orders?"

Chunhyang, who came back to herself at these words, grew even more spiteful and spoke up.

"Magistrate, listen well. If the king knows you've committed the crime of tormenting an innocent person, then you too will be punished. So hurry up and kill me."

"What's this! There's no reasoning with you. See here! Lock Chunhyang in the jail this instant!"

5
Chunhyang is imprisoned

p.36

Chunhyang emerged with a pillory around her neck and Wolmae immediately and frantically rushed forward, clung to her daughter's neck, and cried.

"Oh, what's this! What has my daughter done to be made to wear this pillory? Oh, her mistake was to be born a gisaeng's daughter, wasn't it? Chunhyang, get ahold of yourself. Get ahold of yourself!"

Chunhyang entered the jail and the cold wind blew in through the broken window, and insects crawled through the cracks in the crumbling wall. Wolmae and Hyangdan went home, and Chunhyang, who was all alone, felt sorry for herself and could only cry.

"What crime have I committed? I didn't steal

rice to eat from the country's stores of grain, yet why am I whipped? I didn't kill anyone, yet why do I have to wear this pillory? How unfair, how sorrowful…"

p.37

Chunhyang wept and barely managed to fall asleep. Rain poured down as the night deepened, and the cries of the birds in the night sounded like the cries of ghosts, startling Chunhyang awake. Just then, a fortune teller was passing by outside the jail. From the way he used a cane as he went, it seemed as if he couldn't see what was in front of him.

"Excuse me."

"Who's there?"

"It's Chunhyang."

"Chunhyang? If you're Chunhyang, you're

the prettiest girl in Namwon, aren't you? But what are you calling to me for?"

"I had a frightening dream and I wanted to ask you to interpret it, and I was also wondering when my lord would come to find me."

The fortune teller heard her words and read her fortune for her.

"When will the virtuous woman Seong Chunhyang, who lives in Namwon in Jeolla-do Province, get out of this jail, and when will Lee Mongryong, who lives in Hanyang, arrive here?"

The fortune teller finished his divination and shook the container with which he told fortunes so that it clinked.

"Oho, very good, very good. Your husband who's gone to Hanyang will come here within a month and all your life's sorrows will be resolved."

p.39

Hearing this, Chunhyang's voice grew a little brighter.

"How wonderful it would be if that were to happen."

"No, it will certainly happen. Hold on just a little longer."

As the fortune teller was saying this, a crow flew over from somewhere, crying, "Caw! Caw!" Feeling unsettled, Chunhyang waved her hand at the bird with a swish and sent it flying away.

"Oh, crow, you've come to catch me, haven't you!"

"No! A crow crying means that something will happen to resolve all your life's sorrows, so don't worry too much."

At last, Chunhyang let out a sigh and her worries were assuaged.

6

Mongryong becomes a secret royal inspector

p.40

Meanwhile, Mongryong, who had gone to Hanyang, was hard at work, doing nothing but studying day and night. At first, he missed Chunhyang and did nothing but sleep in his room. But Chunhyang appeared in his dreams, and seeing her worry, he pulled himself together.

Just then, things were going well throughout the land, and the news reached him that the state examination would be held. Mongryong took his books and entered the testing grounds, where all the cleverest people in the entire country were gathered. Fortunately, the question that was asked was one he knew well, and with his excellent penmanship and knowledge, he was first to write and submit his answer.

Just as he'd hoped, Mongryong won first place in the state examination and became a secret royal inspector of Jeolla-do Province.

p.41

Emerging with the mapae (horse requisition tablet) he received from the king, Mongryong looked like a tiger from the heart of the mountains.

After returning home and greeting his parents, Mongryong prepared to leave. In order to conceal the fact that he was a secret royal inspector, he wore the clothes of a poor man. To anyone's eyes, he looked just like a beggar. And he carried a shabby bag, and within it he hid his mapae.

Mongryong leisurely made his way down to Namwon. He wanted to see Chunhyang quickly, but as a secret royal inspector, it was also important to do his job of finding out how the people were living and what they were thinking, and so he listened attentively to the farmers as they sang or talked.

When Mongryong had reached the outskirts of Namwon, a farmer was there, smoking tobacco as he rested for a moment. Mongryong asked the farmer a question.

"Is it true that Chunhyang serves the new magistrate as his mistress, and that she's taking bribes and tormenting the people?"

The farmer was angry and asked Mongryong, "Where are you from?"

"What does it matter where I'm from?"

p.42

"What does it matter? Do they not have eyes and ears where you come from? Right now, Chunhyang has been whipped and is in jail because she said she wouldn't be his mistress, so what the devil are you talking about! If a beggar like you keeps sullying Chunhyang's name, you'll starve to death. And that Master Lee or Master Sam, or whoever it is who went to Hanyang, I heard he suddenly stopped sending news once he got there. How can a person like that work in the government!"

Mongryong stopped talking to the farmer and turned around dismally. Just then, a child came by, talking to himself.

"What's the date today? How many days will it take to get to Hanyang? What happened to poor Chunhyang, locked up in jail? Why doesn't Master Lee contact her? How can noblemen be so cold-hearted?"

"Hey there, child. Where have you come from?"

"From Namwon."

"Where are you going?"

"To Hanyang."

"Why are you going there?"

"I'm bringing a letter from Chunhyang to Lee Mongryong's home."

"Let me see that letter for a moment."

p.43

"Why are you asking to see the letter of another man's wife?"

"I might be able to help you, mightn't I? It's not as if the letter will disappear if I read it, so let me have a look."

The child thought that what Mongryong said seemed true, so he gave him the letter. Mongryong opened it quickly and it was clearly in Chunhyang's handwriting. As there was no way to find something with which to write a letter in prison, she had bitten her fingertip and the writing was in her blood.

p.44

I haven't had news from you in so long, ever since we parted. Are you doing well with your parents, my husband? I've been imprisoned for refusing to serve the new magistrate. I might die at any moment, so I bid you farewell with this letter.

Looking at Chunhyang's letter, Mongryong began to shed tears without even realizing it. The child, seeing this, thought it was strange and asked for the letter back.

"Master Lee is my friend. I've promised to meet him in Namwon tomorrow, so let's go together."

"I don't want to. Give me the letter."

The child grabbed at Mongryong's clothes and pulled, and the mapae fell out of Mongryong's bag.

"You rascal! If you tell anyone you saw this mapae, you won't survive it."

Mongryong got a promise from the child that he would keep his secret, and he went on to Namwon.

7

Mongryong appears as a beggar

p.45

Around the time the sun set, Mongryong arrived at Chunhyang's house. As he went inside, Wolmae was drawing water and setting it aside to pray to the heavens.

"Oh lord, oh lord, please save Chunhyang, my one and only daughter. Take pity on us and please have Lee Mongryong, who went to Hanyang, pass the state examination quickly."

Seeing Wolmae praying, Mongryong grew choked up.

"*I thought it was thanks to my ancestors that I passed the state examination, but it turns out it was thanks to my mother-in-law!*"

"Is someone in there?"

Mongryong shouted loudly and went inside.

"Who is it?"

"It's me."

"And who would 'me' be?"

"It's Mr. Lee."

p.46

"Mr. Lee? Oh, are you the son of Mr. Lee from the next village over?"

"Oho, mother. Have you forgotten your son-in-law's voice?"

"Who is that? My goodness! Look at you. Where have you been to only just be coming back now? Have you heard about Chunhyang and come to save her? Come in, quickly now."

Wolmae spoke with surprise in her voice. But when she set a candle down and looked carefully at Mongryong, she saw he looked like the most wretched beggar she had ever seen.

"What on earth is this appearance of yours?"

"Mother, once one thing goes wrong in a nobleman's life, it's beyond what words can describe. I went to Hanyang, but my path to entering government service was blocked and my family fortune was all lost. I came here thinking I might get a little money from Chunhyang, but I see things are the same here, as well."

Hearing this, Wolmae was dumbfounded and couldn't speak. She was so angry that she grabbed Mongryong's nose and twisted it.

"You cold-hearted man! There was no news

of you after you left, but our Chunhyang still believed in your promise to come back and take her with you, and waited only for you to pass the state examination. How do you intend to save her now!"

"Mother, I'm starving. Give me something to eat first."

"What? What did you say? I've no food to give to you."

p.47

At that moment, Hyangdan, who was returning from meeting Chunhyang at the jail, heard Mongryong's voice and ran quickly inside to greet him.

"Master, I, Hyangdan, greet you kindly. Did you have a safe journey, coming all this way?"

Seeing Mongryong, whom her mistress Chunhyang had missed so much, Hyangdan was so happy that tears began to stream from her eyes. And then she went into the kitchen. She made up a table with some leftover rice, soy sauce, and kimchi, then filled a cup with cold water and brought it all over. Mongryong poured the rice and side dishes together and ate it all up frantically. Hyangdan thought of her mistress then, but couldn't cry out loud and swallowed back her tears.

"Hyangdan, don't cry. You don't think Chunhyang will truly die, do you? If she's committed no crime, she'll surely be released."

Thinking of Chunhyang suffering in jail, Mongryong was heartbroken.

"Hyangdan, clear the table now. Mother, let's go to see Chunhyang."

Just then, they heard the bell signaling dawn. Mongryong followed behind Hyangdan and they arrived at the jail.

"Chunhyang!"

As soon as Chunhyang heard Mongryong's voice, she was startled out of sleep.

"Is this… a dream? I hear my husband's voice."

p.48

Mongryong called out to Chunhyang a little louder.

"Chunhyang, wake up and look at me. I've come."

"Come? Who has come?"

With an irritated voice, Wolmae spoke to Chunhyang.

"I'm not sure that your husband has come, but a beggar certainly has."

Chunhyang approached Mongryong and grasped his hand through the bars; she couldn't breathe, and for some time, she simply cried wordlessly. Getting ahold of herself, Chunhyang looked closely and saw that Mongryong's appearance was so pitiful that it was beyond compare.

p.49

"My husband, I'm not saddened that I should die, but how on earth did you come to look like this?"
"It's alright, Chunhyang. Don't worry. A person's fate is decided by the heavens; surely you won't die, will you?"
Hearing this, Chunhyang called out to her mother.
"Mother, all our efforts have been for naught. My life became a pitiful one, but even after I die, you mustn't hate my husband. Sell the silk clothing that I wore and buy clothes for my husband. Sell my silver hairpin and my ring, too, and buy him a hat and shoes. Even if I'm gone, please look after my husband."
This time, she grabbed her husband's hand and asked a favor of him.
"My husband, tomorrow is Magistrate Byeon's birthday. At his birthday celebration, he'll call for me and whip me again. If I'm whipped any more, I won't be able to survive. If I die, please bury me yourself. And if I do die, my poor mother will have no blood relatives remaining. If you think of my mother as you would of me and look after her, even if I die, I'll repay your kindness."

p.50

Chunhyang finished speaking and sobbed bitterly.
"Don't cry, Chunhyang. It's been said that there's a way out of even the most desperate of situations. Just trust me and wait."
Mongryong wanted to reveal that he had become a secret royal inspector, but he couldn't. He'd intended not to speak to Chunhyang and only to look at her, but he grew so frustrated that he couldn't bear it.

Mongryong comforted the crying Chunhyang, and after he sent Wolmae and Hyangdan back home, he climbed up Gwanghallu Pavilion. Behind him, the administrators who attended to the secret royal inspector in his duties quietly followed along.
"Tomorrow is the magistrate's birthday celebration. When the mood reaches its highest peak, I'll reveal my position, so all of you wait too and don't attract anyone's attention."

8
Here comes the secret royal inspector!

p.51

The next day, the administrators from the neighboring villages descended on Namwon to celebrate Magistrate Byeon's birthday. There were various fruits, precious liquors, and food laid out at the banquet, and to one side, gisaengs were dancing along to music. Mongryong, who had been watching from outside the door, wanted to go in immediately and punish all of them, but he held back his anger and leisurely strolled through.
"See here. Let me beg for some alcohol and snacks at this fine celebration."
As Magistrate Byeon had already forbid beggars from entering, constables blocked Mongryong from making his way inside. At that moment, the magistrate from Unbong saw Mongryong and made a request of Magistrate Byeon.
"Although that beggar's clothes aren't anything special, he seems like a nobleman, so let's sit him at the very end there and give

him some liquor."
As soon as Magistrate Byeon, pretending to be generous, permitted it, Mongryong sat beside the magistrate from Unbong. In front of the other guests had been laid various liquors and foods, but the only thing at his own table was a single cup of rice wine.

p.52

He kicked at his table with his foot and grabbed one of the beef ribs that had been placed on the table for Unbong.
"Let me have some of these ribs."
As Mongryong was eating away at the ribs loudly and impolitely, Unbong spoke to Magistrate Byeon.
"Magistrate, can an enjoyable celebration really be had without a poem? Let's write some verses in rhyme."
"That's good, Unbong. What character should we use to write with?"
"Magistrate, let's try writing with the two characters with the sound of "go," one meaning "high" and one meaning "flesh.""
Just then, Mongryong, who had been listening, stood and spoke up.
"Thanks to my parents, I've read a few books myself ever since I was a child. I would feel sorry to be greeted at this fine party and just be on my way, so let me try composing a verse."
Before anyone else could finish writing their verses, Mongryong wrote down a few characters and stood up quickly from his seat.

p.53

Tasty liquor in golden cups is the blood of the commoners,
Fine food on dishes of jade is the flesh of the commoners.
When the candle drips wax, the tears of the commoners fall,
And as the music's volume rises, the commoners' cries rise higher.

Magistrate Byeon was drunk and didn't know what Mongryong's poem meant, but Unbong's heart sank in his chest.
"Goodness! This is trouble!"
Unbong stood in a hurry and made to leave without even putting his shoes on properly.
"Unbong. Where are you going?"
"I'm going to the lavatory for a moment."
Several administrators realized that there was trouble and stealthily left, but Magistrate Byeon was unaware and ordered for Chunhyang to be brought in.
Just then, Mongryong gave a signal with his eyes, and the constables who followed him

brought out his mapae and shouted loudly.
"Here comes the secret royal inspector!"

p.54

In that instant, the mood of the joyful
celebration changed. While those working
under Magistrate Byeon were flustered, the
administrators from the other villages were
in a hurry to flee. Magistrate Byeon trembled
and then tried to run to look for a place to
hide. Seeing this, the constables rushed at
him and caught him.
"Oh, I'm dead!"
At that moment, Mongryong appeared in the
clothes of a secret royal inspector and spoke
in a loud voice.
"Lock Magistrate Byeon in the jail
immediately."
And then he decided to ask the crimes of
those imprisoned in the jail and release those
who were innocent.

9
Chunhyang and Mongryong's love is realized

p.56

At last came Chunhyang's turn and
Mongryong asked her crime.
"What is this woman's crime?"
The administrator told him what Chunhyang
had done.
"She's the daughter of the gisaeng Wolmae,
imprisoned for refusing to serve the
magistrate as his mistress."
"If the mother is a gisaeng, then the
daughter is clearly a gisaeng as well. And a
gisaeng must naturally accept to serve the

magistrate; how can she hope to live if she
refuses to serve as his mistress? It's right
that you should die, but if you'll serve as my
mistress, I'll spare your life."
Mongryong rebuked her in hopes of learning
what was in Chunhyang's heart, and
Chunhyang was completely dumbounded.
"Each magistrate who comes here is the
same, aren't they! Listen up, inspector. Does
the green pine tree change its color when it
snows? There's not a chance that I'll change
my mind, so hurry up and kill me."

p.57

Mongryong couldn't stand it any longer; he
took a jade ring out of his pocket and gave it
to the administrator.
"Give this to Chunhyang."
Chunhyang took the ring and saw that it was
the same jade ring she'd given Mongryong
when they had parted. Mongryong spoke to
Chunhyang, who was shocked.
"Chunhyang, lift your head and look at me."
Chunhyang raised her head and saw that
the inspector who was sat there was her
husband, who had come to find her disguised
as a beggar.
"Do you recognize me? It's me, your husband
for whom you've waited. Chunhyang."

p.58

For a moment, Chunhyang pondered if this was a dream. Then she collected herself and looked at Mongryong, and tears fell from her eyes in great drops like beads. Mongryong went to Chunhyang and held her tightly. Wolmae and Hyangdan, who saw all this, danced with joy, and the villagers who had come to watch were as happy as if it all were happening to them.

After sending Chunhyang and her mother home, Mongryong checked over everything at the government office until late into the night, and when it became dawn, he went to find Chunhyang. Touching Mongryong's face and holding his hand, Chunhyang cried for some time.

"Stop crying. Didn't I tell you that at the end of difficulties comes happiness? From now on, we'll never be separated, so don't cry. Let's live together forever, like we first promised."

Chunhyang and Mongryong gazed into each other's faces until the day brightened, sharing everything they hadn't been able to say to one another until then.

The next day, Mongryong took Chunhyang, her mother, and Hyangdan, and headed for Hanyang. They were praised unendingly by so many people.

Afterwards, the king praised Chunhyang, who had risked her life to maintain her chastity, and gave her the title of a "Lady of Virtue." And Mongryong held several government positions, and after he retired from the government, had daughters and sons with Chunhyang and lived a long, happy, and good life.

Darakwon Korean Readers

춘향전 The Story of Chunhyang

Adapted by Kim Yu Mi, Bae Se Eun
Translated by Jamie Lypka
First Published June, 2021
Publisher Chung Kyudo
Editor Lee Suk-hee, Baek Da-heuin, Park Inkyung
Cover Design Yoon Ji-young
Interior Design Yoon Hyun-ju
Illustrator SOUDAA
Voice Actor Shin So-yun, Kim Rae-whan

Published by Darakwon Inc.
Darakwon Bldg., 211 Munbal-ro, Paju-si, Gyeonggi-do
Republic of Korea 10881
Tel : 02-736-2031 Fax : 02-732-2037
(Marketing Dept. ext.: 250~252, Editorial Dept. ext.: 420~426)

Price 9,000 won

ISBN 978-89-277-3270-9 14710
978-89-277-3259-4 (set)

Visit the Darakwon homepage to learn about our other
publications and promotions and to download the contents of
the MP3 format.

http://www.darakwon.co.kr
http://koreanbooks.darakwon.co.kr